A RAIN-DARKENED POND IN WILLAMETTE NATIONAL FOREST

FIRST TINTS OF FALL AT QUAKING ASPEN SWAMP, OREGON

LOW CLOUDS INVADING A VALLEY NEAR CASCADE PASS

TANGLED ROOTS OF A HEMLOCK STUMP NEAR CRATER LAKE

SUMMIT RIDGES OF THE NORTHERN CASCADES

A CLIFF-EDGE TRAIL IN ROGUE RIVER NATIONAL FOREST

FROST ENCRUSTING A TUMBLE OF VOLCANIC ROCK AT LAVA BUTTE, OREGON

LAKE VIVIANE'S HEADWALL AGLOW AT SUNRISE

THE CASCADES

THE AMERICAN WILDERNESS/TIME-LIFE BOOKS/NEW YORK

BY RICHARD L. WILLIAMS
AND THE EDITORS OF TIME-LIFE BOOKS

TIME-LIFE BOOKS

FOUNDER: Henry R. Luce 1898-1967

Editor-in-Chief: Hedley Donovan
Chairman of the Board: Andrew Heiskell
President: James R. Shepley
Group Vice President: Rhett Austell

Vice Chairman: Roy E. Larsen

MANAGING EDITOR: Jerry Korn
Assistant Managing Editors: Ezra Bowen,
David Maness, Martin Mann, A. B. C. Whipple
Planning Director: Oliver E. Allen
Art Director: Sheldon Cotler
Chief of Research: Beatrice T. Dobie
Director of Photography: Melvin L. Scott
Senior Text Editor: Diana Hirsh
Assistant Art Director: Arnold C. Holeywell
Assistant Chief of Research: Myra Mangan

PUBLISHER: Joan D. Manley
General Manager: John D. McSweeney
Business Manager: John Steven Maxwell
Sales Director: Carl G. Jaeger
Promotion Director: Paul R. Stewart
Public Relations Director: Nicholas Benton

THE AMERICAN WILDERNESS

SERIES EDITOR: Robert Morton
Editorial Staff for *The Cascades:*
Text Editors: Peter Janssen, Philip W. Payne
Picture Editors: Kaye Neil, Mary Y. Steinbauer
Designer: Charles Mikolaycak
Staff Writers: Carol Clingan,
Simone D. Gossner, Lee Hassig
Chief Researcher: Martha T. Goolrick
Researchers: Muriel Clarke, Doris Coffin,
Helen M. Hinkle, Beatrice Hsia,
Patricia Kiesewetter, Gretchen Wessels,
Editha Yango
Design Assistant: Vincent Lewis

Editorial Production
Production Editor: Douglas B. Graham
Assistant Production Editor: Gennaro C. Esposito
Quality Director: Robert L. Young
Assistant Quality Director: James J. Cox
Copy Staff: Rosalind Stubenberg (chief),
Barbara Quarmby, Mary Ellen Slate,
Florence Keith
Picture Department: Dolores A. Littles,
Joan Lynch
Traffic: Feliciano Madrid

Valuable assistance was given by the following
departments and individuals of Time Inc.:
Editorial Production, Norman Airey; Library,
Benjamin Lightman; Picture Collection,
Doris O'Neil; Photographic Laboratory, George
Karas; TIME-LIFE News Service, Murray J.
Gart; Correspondent Jane Estes (Seattle).

The Author: To write this book, Richard L. Williams spent an entire summer in the Cascades, traveling more than 10,000 miles on foot, on horseback and by car. For Williams, who was born in Seattle, this trip "home" was his second in recent years —he also wrote *The Northwest Coast* for The American Wilderness series. He has been a writer, editor and correspondent with the *Seattle Times,* Dell Publishing Co., and TIME and LIFE magazines. As a staff member of TIME-LIFE BOOKS he was the editor of the LIFE Library of Photography and the 27-volume Foods of the World series.

The Cover: The graceful cone of Mount Saint Helens gleams in the parting rays of an October sunset that has already abandoned the lesser ridges and clouded valleys of the southern Cascades.

Contents

A Forested Wall of Mountains

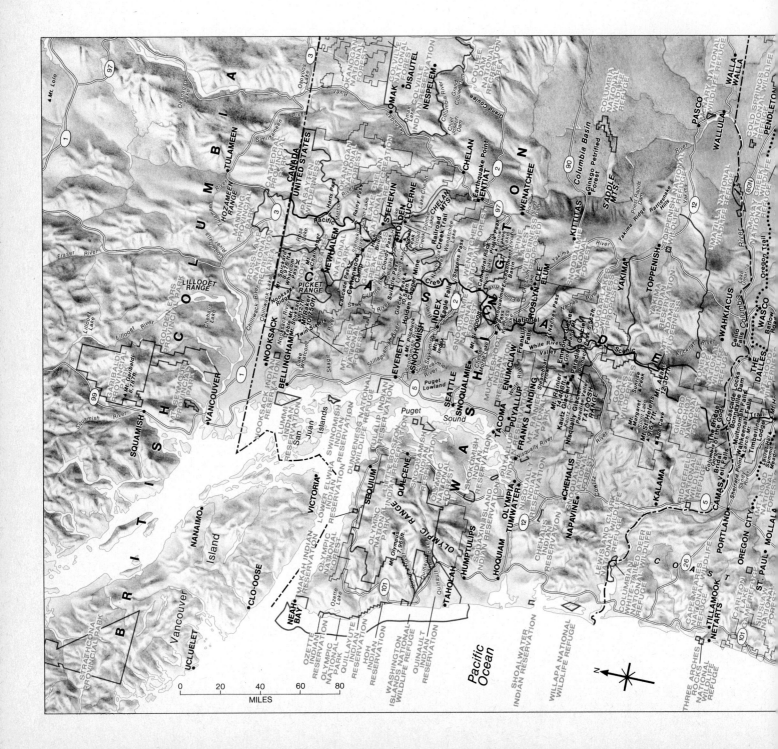

The Cascade Range forms a mountain wall stretching more than 600 miles from Canada into northern California. An unbroken chain of 16 National Forests is outlined in light red on the map. The range's many National Parks, Wildlife Refuges, Indian Reservations —as well as Wildernesses and Primitive Areas within the National Forests—are traced in heavy red.

Rivers and streams appear as blue lines, lakes as white areas bordered in blue. Trails, such as the spectacular Pacific Crest National Scenic Trail, are solid black lines. Dotted lines show historic emigrants' routes. Peaks appear as black triangles; points of special interest as squares; towns as dots. Mountain passes are designated in reversed brackets:) (.

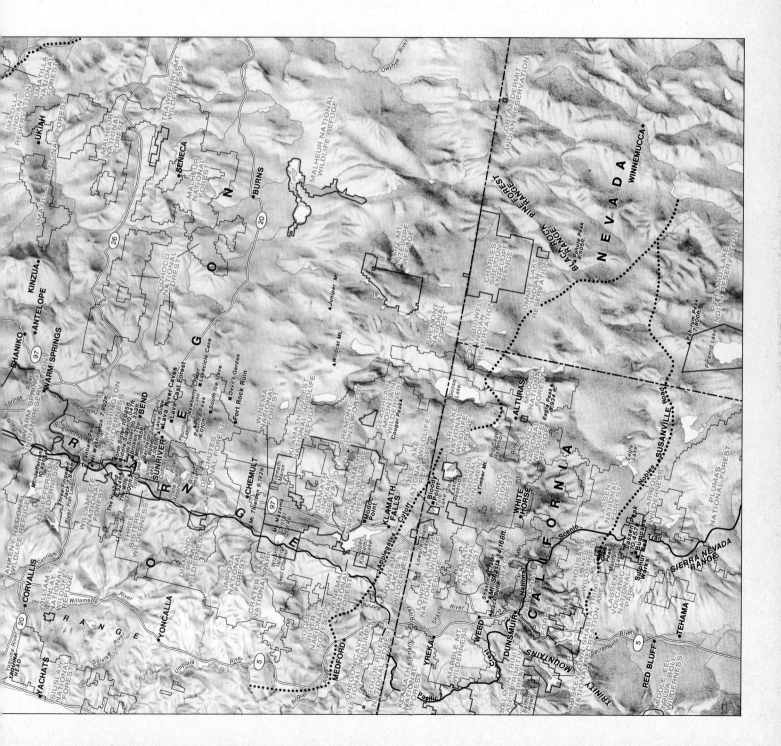

1/ Going Home to the Wilderness

I get away a mile or two from the town into the stillness and solitude of nature, with rocks, trees, weeds, snow about me...and it is as if I had come to an open window.   HENRY DAVID THOREAU/ A WRITER'S JOURNAL

To some people the Cascade Range of the Pacific Northwest is a mountaineering challenge; to others it is a skiing paradise, a laboratory of geological marvels, a cornucopia of timber and mining resources. To still others, it is a sacred region of wild plants and wild creatures, to see but not to touch, a wilderness to be kept inviolate of any sound louder than fish slapping water.

But when I think of the Cascades, I cannot muster a simple word-association response because of the kaleidoscope of images that keeps forming and reforming in my mind. I was born here, though for a long time I have lived a continent's width away. When I think back, I remember first the trail to an alpine lake where I once counted 40 different wild flowers in a quarter of a mile. In the lens of my memory, the trail is wonderfully springy underfoot, moist and black and deeply cushioned by many seasons' worth of fallen hemlock needles. A few yards ahead two yearling deer, their coats clean and light tan, stop and look at me before crossing the path, no sign of fright in their eyes.

At the end of another trail at Lake Chelan, high among the peaks, I stare into the choppy water and reflect that the bottom of the submerged glaciated valley, 1,605 feet down, is actually 509 feet *below* sea level. Many miles away, on the south bank of the Columbia River, I look skyward and feel the wayward mist from Multnomah Falls, which pours out of a rock cleft in a ribbon that comes 620 feet straight down.

Then, traveling west, across the brown rock of the Columbia Plateau to revisit these mountains, I am confronted by the sawtoothed silhouette that is their horizon—a succession of carbon-blue mountains studded with snowy volcanic peaks. And I think of the pioneers who saw the same sight more than 100 years earlier. To them the Cascades must have seemed a heartbreaking final barrier to the promised lands, planted in the path of prairie schooners pulled by weary oxen.

Memory takes hold again. And in a sidehill grove of statuesque pines, I hike to the source of the mysterious Metolius River: it boils up right out of the ground, then glides away, past miniature green islands ablaze with blossoms. At the crest of a long slope thickly grown with Shasta red firs and matronly, sweet-smelling sugar pines, I peer through the treetops and get a first, astonished look into Crater Lake, so round and blue and large that the brain wants to reject the evidence of the eyes.

I grew up on the western side of the Cascades in the Puget Sound lowland where, 15,000 years before, the last of the great glaciers scalloped out hundreds of peaceable harbors and inlets. The cities that grew there made their living mainly from wood—the seemingly inexhaustible stands of Douglas fir that robed the nearby foothill slopes. One summer I made a living that way too. In a noisy mill built out over the water on pilings and smelling of fresh sawdust and the tide, I stood in front of a guillotine-like saw, my navel pressed against a steel plate. Every few seconds a fir board slammed onto the plate; the saw cut the wood, and I snatched away and stacked the lengths, which were destined to be boards for somebody's floor. After work I walked home a mile uphill, rubbing a sore arm and glimpsing Mount Pilchuck, a minor Cascade peak, pink as a small Vesuvius at sunset in the eastern sky.

Then, as now, the inhabitants of that area led a literally sheltered life, protected from the worst furies of the elements by being enclosed between the Cascades just to the east and the Olympic Range across the sound to the west. Even when fog, rain or snow made the mountains invisible, as they often were, we felt their mitigating presence. And when a great volcano like Mount Rainier reappeared after many days of sulking behind clouds, everyone felt cheered and comforted. Perhaps the mountains produced a kind of insularity among those living at their feet. Yet to me they provided a most fundamental, if unconscious, sense of security. It was like living in the hollow of the cupped hand of God.

If I had known then all that I know now about the Cascades, I doubt that life near them would have been any more enjoyable. As it was, traveling light intellectually, unencumbered by the facts of geology, geography and natural history, I ventured frequently and innocently into the wilderness at our backs. I fished in turbulent streams that issue from the heights, hiked through moistly fragrant forests to remote high lakes, crossed mountain passes to hunt pheasant in the tawny fields of the semiarid eastern slope, and skied the long, steep sides of Mount Baker and Mount Rainier. I tagged along after my father on many early trips; he was no earth scientist either, but a pragmatic fishing and hunting specialist. He knew when and where the fish were likely to bite or the ruffed grouse likely to emerge from cover, even if he barely knew one rock or tree from another.

He taught me how to build a fire, while crouched over cedar shavings in pouring rain, and—more important to survival—taught me that these thick forests and sheer rock faces could be dangerous. They were full of places where a misstep on a slippery rock could get you soaked or hurt, if not killed. The higher one traveled, I learned, the greater the danger—mainly from avalanches in the snowpack, which is so deep much of it remains on the heights the year round. I heard one harrowing story about two Forest Service rangers out on a summer patrol who stopped to chat on a snow slope. Suddenly one of them began moving downhill, as if on an escalator, leaving the other standing where he was, at the edge of an accelerating snowslide. The ranger caught in the avalanche had the presence of mind to fling himself face-down downhill and "swim," breaststroke fashion, trying to keep on top of the torrent of snow. The avalanche swept him hundreds of yards downslope before his companion reached him. He was not deeply buried but he had been stripped as naked as a potato in a tumbling machine. Though cut and bruised, he was still alive.

In my youthful acceptance of things, I assumed the Cascades had been there forever. In fact, they are relatively young, a set of brutally uplifted, folded, faulted, erupted, weathered and glaciated rocks only about 25 million years old. The great volcanoes that dominate the region, towering a mile above their surrounding peaks, are even younger, less than a million years of age. All the rock types are present: the sedimentary, formed on the ocean floor before the range rose out of the sea; the igneous, melted in the crucible of the earth's inner heat; and finally the metamorphic, alchemized underground by tremendous heat and pressure. Some of the rocks, thousands of feet above sea level, bear chambered shells and other marine fossils as evidence of their sub-

A hungry mule deer, blocked by deep snow from its usual forage, roams the banks of a stream in Washington's Tumwater Canyon.

marine origins. Thousands of feet down rest the remnants of an earlier mountain range, long since subsided or ground away.

The entire range stretches from Canada into northern California. In all, it measures more than 600 miles long and from 30 to 80 miles wide, and is broken once, by the Columbia River Gorge. Early pioneers named the range after the Cascades—swirling white-water rapids in the middle of the gorge where the Columbia once took a sudden drop of 20 feet; the rapids are now underwater behind Bonneville Dam. The range contains thousands of lakes, about 900 glaciers (more than in all the rest of the United States), hundreds of peaks (including Mount Rainier, 14,408 feet, in the north, and Mount Shasta, 14,162 feet, in the south) and an unbroken string of 16 National Forests, some sprawling over more than a million acres.

Climatologically, the Cascades help serve as a shield for the interior of the continent. That shield effect is the most significant fact of the natural life of the Northwest. Clouds sweeping in from the ocean deflect upward, first against the Olympics and then the Cascades. The clouds cool as they rise, and release virtually all their moisture as snow and rain on the mountains' western slope.

The results of this moisture-trapping function are dramatically visible—and abrupt. Within miles on either side of the crest, the Cascades change from green on the west to brown on the east. The western slope is dominated by the great Douglas fir and the western hemlock, which require heavy rainfall and stand in thick, wet underbrush. The eastern slope is covered with dry ponderosa and other pines, which barely survive on only a few inches of rain a year. They stand in a bleached litter of their own dry twigs and needles.

The amount of precipitation on either side of the watershed also has a fundamental effect on the people who live throughout the region. If the mountains get an unusually heavy snowfall, some highway passes are closed and east-west travel is disrupted. Too light a snowpack, however, will cause water shortages the following summer.

The Cascades are so vast and varied and rugged that it is virtually impossible to get a panoramic impression of them, from the Fraser River in British Columbia all the way down to their southern tip at the still-steaming volcano of Lassen Peak in northern California. In December 1968, a Seattle sailplane enthusiast named Cecil Craig made a heroic attempt. He prudently avoided trying to glide down the North Cascades, where a white-capped sea of ferocious peaks offers no safe place to land. Instead, after casting loose from his tow plane, he flew his World

War II glider south from the crowning eminence of Mount Rainier, and then climbed to 30,800 feet—twice the height of Rainier's summit crater. Taking advantage of rising, cooling waves at each of the other volcanoes and helped by a southward-flowing jet stream, he soared at 24,000 feet over Mount Adams, swooped across the Columbia River, passed over Mount Hood at 20,500 feet, dropped to 17,000 feet at Mount Jefferson and rose again to 24,000 feet over South Sister.

After five and a half hours of roller-coastering on thermal currents, Craig came to earth in a snowy meadow just east of the rim of wind-whipped Crater Lake. He was within sight of his goal, Lassen Peak, and he felt exultant. In soaring around and over all those peaks, Craig said, "You feel in imagination like a bird, the glider wings seeming to come right out of your shoulders, and the only sound you hear is the wind whistling over your canopy." The temperature was 10° below zero, and a 50-mile-an-hour wind was blowing at the 8,000-foot level where he landed. A rescue party found him the same night.

Cecil Craig's eagle's-eye view along hundreds of miles of the Cascades was dramatic but, for me, too detached. He could never scratch the surface of the land, let alone hear a waterfall, come close to an animal or smell a flower. A more rewarding way to experience the mountains is to hike parts of the Pacific Crest National Scenic Trail (called the Cascade Crest in Washington and the Oregon Skyline in Oregon). Its total length, from Canada to Mexico, is 2,404 miles.

The Cascade portion, from British Columbia south to Mount Lassen, is about 1,200 miles long, providing a magnificent sequence of encounters with animals and birds, alpine meadows and lakes. In some stretches, it is good and tough. Most of the trail lies at 7,000 feet or higher, and generally it is exhaustingly steep. On north slopes, deep snowbanks occasionally obliterate the trail until late summer—when the first storm of the next winter may arrive any evening. But to walk along the trail is to intrude on some of the wildest areas in North America. And though three or four million people live within perhaps an hour's drive of the trail, here the human bootprint seldom, if ever, mixes with the tracks of bears and deer, cougars and mountain goats.

For all my childhood excursions into the northern Cascades, I remained a stranger to many other parts of the range. But I suspect anyone's view of the Cascades might depend on where in the region he lived —and, like mine, might be parochial as well as possessive. Around Everett and Seattle, we had never heard of Broken Top Mountain near

Bend, Oregon, any more than people around Bend were aware of Mount Pilchuck near Everett and Seattle. Last summer, wanting to enlarge my own view, I sought a base in browner pastures, east of the crest, where the countryside is not drenched but parched.

I found it at Sunriver, Oregon (population 270, elevation 4,200 feet). A new town on the site of the Army's old Camp Abbot, 15 miles south of Bend, it is only half an hour by car from the central Oregon Cascades, and less than a day from any other point in the mountains. Sunriver has its own share of wilderness: five meandering miles of the Deschutes River flowing through colonies of aspen and groves of ponderosa, or yellow pine, all bushy-needled and clad in thick, cinnamon-colored bark patterned like reptile skin.

That summer—as usual—Bend was a likely place to be chilly at night. In fact, there have only been eight dates since they started keeping records in 1901 when Bend has not recorded a frost—which makes it difficult to grow tomatoes but easy to grow sagebrush. On many a bracing July and August dawn, when I headed out into the mountains, the grass at Sunriver glistened in the sun like acres of frappéed crème de menthe. On those mornings the yellow-pine chipmunks and the Cascades golden-mantled ground squirrels, which must outnumber the human population a thousandfold, seemed to scamper through the trees with unusual speed, as if to keep warmer in their hunt for seeds.

Except for a few shrews and baby bats, these are the smallest mammals I have met in the Cascades and, with no exception, are the most fun to watch. Both are less than a foot long, both carry their tails perkily high and both are tawny-colored, much paler than their relatives in denser, more humid forests. Both species also stuff food into cheek pouches, or stand erect, nibbling at a morsel held in the front paws.

But for all their resemblance to each other, they are easily distinguished: the chipmunk's light-and-dark stripes run right to its nose, while the ground squirrel's stripes stop at its neck. The chipmunk likes to take to the trees to get its food, while the squirrel rummages around for the same seeds on the ground. The chipmunk hoards as many as 35,000 seeds in its burrow for the winter, while the ground squirrel in torpor simply lives off its accumulated fat. I've never seen either kind get caught, but a long list of predators, from falcons and hawks to martens and coyotes, keeps their numbers down. In a chase on the ground, most enemies would have little hope of catching one of the speedy rodents. Many are killed, however, while they are hibernating.

As a native of Seattle, where it is always raining or getting ready

Columbia tiger lilies nod gracefully beside a mountain trail in Washington. The plant often grows among coarse bracken ferns, whose roots help to shield the lily's edible bulb from the depredations of marauding rodents.

to rain or getting over a rain, I was surprised that I liked the dry landscape of the southeast Cascades. Between the high peaks the countryside seems round instead of jagged. And because of the sparse rainfall, the forests look more like parks than thickets. The relative absence of underbrush allows you to get a really good look at the native animals and birds: a mule deer, an osprey or a bald eagle, once seen, is in view a long time before fading into the trees. So is a shy coyote, trotting along a road or trail but somehow never coming toward you (for it has usually seen you first), before it disappears into the sagebrush, tail and head down. (The animal's name, by the way, is pronounced *KYE-oat* in these parts, not *kye-OH-tee*.) Signs of relatively recent volcanism are everywhere: the minivolcanoes called cinder cones, huge flows of glinting black obsidian, flatlands carpeted with pink pumice, fields of lava looking as fresh as newly turned black earth.

One hot July day my wife and I crossed one of these lava beds in search of Benham Falls, a long course of rapids in the Deschutes River west of a 500-foot-high cinder cone called Lava Butte. Our trail ended abruptly at a collapsed bridge, so we set out cross country, through tangles of red-twigged manzanita bushes. The falls are only a mile or so from the ruined bridge, but the hike took two hours. As we clambered over blocks of lava and stumbled through marshes ankle-deep in muck, we could hear the water long before we saw it.

The falls were not steep but they were impressive, a place where the placid Deschutes turns quickly into a half-mile maelstrom of white water, rushing through a corridor between tall ponderosas and firs. A thousand years ago the lava bed had thrust the river aside at this point; the falls were made by lava piling up on the bottom. They can be dangerous. A few miles downstream, a young man had drowned the week before. The current carried him into a lava chute leading to an underwater cave, where scuba divers, at some risk, recovered the body.

We stood for a time, looking down at the river, hypnotized by its ceaseless rumbling. On the way back, we saw lizards streaking across the sun-scorched lava ("It's almost as hot as if it just erupted," Mary said) and watched a furtive coyote duck behind a hummock of jumbled rock. The lava was black as night, abrasive to the touch, a wasteland seemingly without end. At times, crossing hollows of that desolate expanse of rock piles, we felt lost—no trail, no vegetation, no horizon, no reference point but the blazing sun. This entire environment seemed out of place on earth, a colorless scene from another, long-dead world.

Far to the north of Benham Falls. I caught sight of the hazy-blue Cascades from the rolling wheat fields of the Columbia Basin. Heading west, I started up into Stevens Pass through apple orchards that were turning the foothills from blossom pink to jade green. I stopped for lunch at a place that bore a familiar far-Northwest welcome sign on the front door—"No shirt, No shoes, No service."

While eating, I remembered a fearsome place in the wilderness, not far from here. When I was growing up we called it The Train Wreck Place. It was marked by an abandoned concrete snowshed, two tracks wide and nearly a mile long, that scarred a steep rock wall high in the Skykomish Valley. (The shed has since been replaced by an eight-mile tunnel that pierces the Cascades at a lower, safer level.) In February 1910, a tremendous storm descended on the Northwest, dropping snow everywhere from the Pacific to Montana, depositing it savagely on the Cascade passes. Drifts and avalanches clogged the tracks. A passenger train and a fast mail from Saint Paul were marooned at Wellington, near Stevens Pass in Washington.

Rotary snowplows were stalled on both ends of the two stranded trains, in slides that had piled boulders and trees, as well as snow, onto long stretches of track. Inside the trains, while the week dragged on, the travelers' mood sank from carefree good cheer to anxiety as the reassurance of food and liquor ran out. Finally a young male stenographer, secretary to a Great Northern official, turned from staring out a window at the ominous-looking peaks, and read aloud a stanza from Byron that the railroad had quoted in a travel brochure:

Above me are the Alps,
The palaces of nature, whose vast walls
Have pinnacled in clouds their snowy scalps,
And throned Eternity in icy halls
Of cold sublimity, where forms and falls
The avalanche—the thunderbolt of snow!

His melancholy recitation could hardly have cheered his half-frozen companions, and it was all too prophetic. That night the snows turned to rain. Lightning stabbed at the peaks, and thunder cannonaded in the canyon. Far above the tracks, the burden of snow on Windy Mountain gave way and roared downhill. Snapping off trees and gathering up great rocks, the avalanche swept across the tracks and on down the canyon. When it had passed, the trains had vanished, along with the snowplows and everything else in its 1,400-foot-wide path.

On an August evening, three shark-fin crags throw lengthening shadows across old snowfields on a north slope of 6,925-foot Chikamin Peak in the Alpine Lakes country of Washington. The ground cover of red heather and the lone, wind-battered alpine fir are typical of timberline vegetation in the rugged north-central Cascades.

This was the worst avalanche in railroad history, killing 97 people but miraculously sparing a score of others. And it showed, if proof were needed, what terrors inhabit the wilderness. It may also have reminded some of the old and still-surviving pioneers, who had crossed the Cascades by wagon train in the middle of the previous century, how generous Providence had been to them, letting them struggle their way over this great mountain barrier and get down the other side alive.

After lunch I continued on up to Stevens Pass to seek out a far gentler memory—a small waterfall that I had hiked to many times and many years before. As I neared the pass, I wondered if Eagle Falls was still unspoiled; in fact, I was unaccountably worried that the falls might not even be there now.

When I was a boy, Eagle Falls seemed a secret, sacred place. To get there we took a dusty gravel road that ended well west of the summit, at the decrepit mining town of Index. Then we walked eastward and upward, along the Great Northern tracks that followed the Skykomish River. My father carried the fishing tackle, and the rest of the family strung out behind him, lugging the bedrolls and food. At three-miles-above-Index, as we called it, we scrambled down the railroad embankment into a grove of Christmassy-smelling firs and cedars.

The falls were 20 feet away, where the river churned around an obstacle course of great granite blocks to pause at a big pool before heading down-mountain again. Monolithic Mount Index rose above the trees on the far bank, blocking out the sun most of the day. We fished for rainbow trout, using salmon eggs rather than flies, and when the fish weren't biting we swam in the deep natural pool or sat on high rocks, tossing pieces of bark into the falls to see where they would surface in the quiet water below. Sometimes a deer would come by, drink water from the pool (if we sat very still) and move on. At night, after eating pan-fried rainbow, we slept on beds of cedar boughs.

The sound of tumbling water put us to sleep, but we awakened from time to time to the wail of train whistles from the tracks above. They were the spooky moans of the silk trains, laboring upgrade with throbbing steam engines, rushing perishable raw silk from Japan to the mills in the East, and having right-of-way over all other traffic, including the crack Oriental Limited passenger trains. There were few other signs of civilization. In a dozen visits to Eagle Falls in those years, we rarely saw another hiker or fisherman.

The falls are still there. I found the path, and walked down to the grove. The stony ground was still carpeted with evergreen needles and mosses; the spillway of water was as loud and unruly as I remembered it. Four impassive fishermen were perched on rocks on my side of the falls. I was annoyed at their presence, but they soon departed, two with fish and two without, leaving me with the place to myself. I sat on a rock, tossed cedar twigs into the noisy water, and saw a bush of wild blackberries within arm's reach. A few were ripe, as clean and bittersweet as ever.

I stayed a long time, not really thinking but letting my senses fill up with the wilderness sounds, sights and smells that they had missed for a generation. I wondered about many things. How had Charlie Williams, my father, ever discovered or stumbled upon Eagle Falls in the first place? Why did he keep going back there, and to all the other hard-to-climb streams with Indian names—the Snoqualmie, the Snohomish, the Stillaguamish, the Skagit—that trickled from underneath cloudy glaciers, gathering water and force as they roared down twisting canyons to spill out into the sound? I think I knew why.

At work he was a demon salesman, committed to the high-pressure ethic of the new automobile age, seeing every one of his fellow citizens as a "prospect" for the kind of car that came with brass head lamps, tool chests on the running boards and guy wires running from roof to front fenders. At home he could be a terrible-tempered Mr. Bang, easily infuriated by any family interruption of his meticulous planning of sales calls for the next day. But in the mountains he was a changed man. The rumble of falling water, the size and silences of the great trees and the soaring slopes, seemed to bathe him in peace and patience. He never raised his voice, even if we foolishly snagged a line in a tree branch; and when he urged us to keep low, out of sight of his easily scared fish, it was merely in an urgent whisper. He betrayed his restlessness only in quickly tiring of any spot that was not productive of trout, and wandering mile after arduous mile upstream or down.

I am not short-tempered, as my father ordinarily was. But I too am calmed and refreshed by every visit to high and lonely places, even resentful as he was of any other fisherman or hiker seeking the same solitude. At last I stood up and walked away, grateful that Eagle Falls, not a very important place to anyone else, had not let me down.

Mountains of Fire and Ice

PHOTOGRAPHS BY WILLIAM GARNETT

From various perspectives the dazzling spectrum of land forms known as the Cascades might be at least two or three entirely different ranges. The Cascades do, in fact, combine two distinct but intermingled kinds of mountains. One kind is volcanic, part of a great circle of living cauldrons that rims the Pacific Ocean. In the southern Cascades these volcanoes, the largest between Alaska and Mexico, rise from an undulating forested plateau (pages 34-35). Each stands remote, ethereal, dominant. Even the lesser peaks, like Mount Saint Helens (opposite), soar grandly above the surrounding woods. And real giants like Rainier and Hood do appear immense—some pioneers thought that Mount Hood stood 18,000 feet tall, more than a third higher than the mountain really is.

In the northern part of the range, the volcanoes of Mount Baker (pages 38-39) and Glacier Peak seem to crowd shoulder to shoulder with jagged mountains, the products of buckling and lifting of the earth's crust. This northern massif by itself forms one of the great ranges of America —an overwhelming confusion of high ridges, glaciers, sharp peaks and deep, wild valleys (pages 40-43).

The Cascades first began to take on their present character some five million years ago, when huge shifts in the earth's crust lifted parts of the region into a mountain wall so high that it made its own weather, forcing eastbound clouds from the Pacific to drop most of their moisture on the western slopes. Streams gashed the sides of these new mountains, while volcanic eruptions built tall cones and then gradually layered the land with lava.

During a series of ice ages, mountaintop, or alpine, glaciers formed and cut into peaks and mountain flanks. Some of the ice-scoured volcanoes, meanwhile, often repaired such erosion damage with new eruptions of lava. In the lowlands, mile-thick masses of ice widened valleys into intramountain plains.

Around 12,000 years ago, the frozen oceans retreated and the moist slopes slowly acquired their carpeting of forest. On the major peaks, however, many alpine glaciers remain. A minor climatic change might swell them again into huge rivers of ice that could descend and scour off the forest. And at any time a relatively small shift of the earth's crust could again release the fury of the fiery cones that once covered this country with cinders, ash and lava.

Erosion has deeply scored the flanks of Mount Saint Helens; but later eruptions have rebuilt its symmetrical summit, where snows smooth out any lingering deformities. Lens-shaped clouds hovering above the crest signal the imminent approach of a moist air mass from the Pacific Ocean.

A High and Pleasant Plateau

In a typical south Cascade panorama, tall volcanoes like the Three Sisters and Broken Top (right) or Diamond Peak (page 37) rise from plateaus that are themselves some 5,000 feet above sea level. Throughout the area shown here, known as the Sisters region, much of the land between the peaks is forested with hemlock and Douglas fir standing far enough apart to allow cathedral-aisle vistas between the trunks.

Among the trees lie chains of shallow lakes, like Hosmer (right), which gradually turn into marshes as silt washed from the guardian volcanoes accumulates on their bottoms and plants encroach on their verges.

Elsewhere, the south Cascades present a startling variety of terrain. Rounded summits taper into long, smooth glacial ridges. These in turn give way to moss-banked streams and shaded glens. Then suddenly the trees will end in a desolate lava flow. Just as abruptly, the lava gives way to a gentle meadow. Here and there the earth is honeycombed by volcanic tunnels, so that rivers spring in full flow from the ground, and lakes exist without visible inlets or outlets. One of these lakes fluctuates from 300 to 3,000 acres—while others maintain an unvarying size.

The volcanoes in the south stand like islands in a rolling green sea of forested valleys and ridges. Near Bend, Oregon, on the eastern slope of the range, South Sister (right) and Broken Top (far right) dominate the skyline.

Red and green algae color the surface of Davis Lake near the Sisters region. The lake was formed by a volcano more than 2,000 years ago, when lava, whose frozen waves form the shoreline below, blocked Odell Creek.

Across a gradually sloping plateau, a forest of lodgepole pine sprawls southeastward from Diamond Peak. In glacier-made hollows lie Oldenberg Lake (foreground), the three Bingham lakes and Crescent Lake (far right).

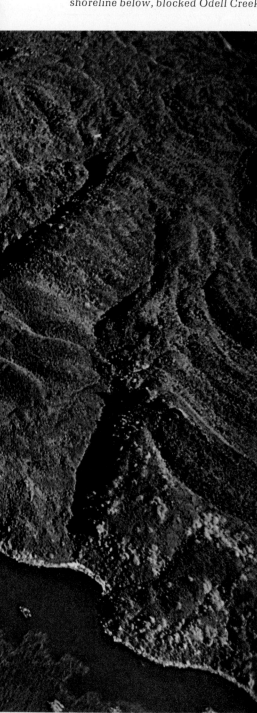

A Profusion of Wild Peaks

The highest and coldest parts of the Cascades lie in the northern region, where peaks like Mount Baker (left) and its saw-toothed companions exist in icy splendor.

Above lower slopes thick in forest, their snowcaps are eternal. The precipitation rate here is one of the greatest in the continental United States. About 80 per cent of the water falls as snow—665 inches a year, but reaching 1,000 inches in spots.

As a result Mount Baker is, ton for ton, the most heavily glaciated of all Cascade volcanoes, with an annual snowfall measuring 80 feet (its eight-month ski season ends officially on the Fourth of July with the Slush Cup, in which competitors try to ski down a slope and across a puddle of melting snow and ice).

These northern mountains, with their razor-edged ridges and sheer slopes, are all the more striking for the abrupt way in which they rise from the sides of deep U-shaped valleys (page 40). All the terrain here —valleys and peaks, ridges and tarns (page 41)—has been shaped by ice, to a greater degree than in the southern Cascades. And here the glaciers are still alive, steadily continuing the work of remodeling the features of the range.

Glaciers seamed with crevasses encase the summit of Mount Baker. At right is a dark streak of shattered rock loosened by the continual effect of frost action and now being carried away on the surface of a great ice river.

The Napeequa River Valley in the Glacier Peak Wilderness was once a V-shaped slash in volcanic rock. Some 20,000 years ago, a rock-studded glacier gouged a U-shaped trough. Rain and the receding glacier's meltwater carved the Napeequa's wandering channel.

Another memento of the last ice age is crescent-shaped Silver Lake, a tarn near the summit of Mount Spickard about one half mile south of the Canadian border. The lake's scooped-out basin and the knife-edged walls above were all sculpted by glacial ice.

From the ocean beyond the distant Olympic Mountains, an afternoon haze blows across the white streak of Puget Sound. Moisture-laden

air crossing the summits of the jumbled peaks may precipitate as rain or snow to continue the inexorable reshaping of the Cascades.

2/ The Pioneers' Vision

Here is no natural pass. You breast the lofty hills and climb them; there is no way around them, no avoiding them, and each succeeding one you fancy to be the dividing ridge of the range. GEORGE CURRY/ 1846

Going up or going down, this was one tough hill. Ranger Warren Olney and I were trying to go up, clawing at rocks that gave way and went clattering down out of sight. We could not get traction with our boots because chunks of rock kept sliding out from underfoot, starting small slides below us. The only way to hang on, and climb higher, was to clutch branches of rhododendron that had gained a roothold on the cliff, or to cling to sturdy stalks of ocean spray, the pliable plant that Indians used as stock for arrows. Halfway to the top, we reached our unlikely objective: a two-foot-thick, rotting cedar stump tilted downhill and incised all around with a deep scar left by rope. We grabbed it, panting. The incline was at least 60°.

"You mean to say oxen and wagons actually came down here?" I asked Warren incredulously.

"Yes, they did, by the hundreds, though they didn't all make it. The emigrants, my own family among them, called this place Laurel Hill," Warren said, "because they mistook the rhododendron for the laurel bushes they had known back East. They called this particular spot the Chute. It was absolutely the worst obstacle on the entire Oregon Trail. This cedar, which they used like a capstan to snub their covered wagons down the Chute, is historic. I've got to bathe the stump in some kind of preservative or it will be gone in a couple more years."

I doubt that anyone who went down the Chute—part of the old Barlow Road sector of the Oregon Trail, leading to the fertile land of the Willamette Valley—ever forgot it. And, unlike us, they all came one way: down. Traveling down the Chute in 1852, one amazed emigrant, E. W. Conyers, wrote in his diary: "The road on this hill is something terrible. It is worn down into the soil from five to seven feet, leaving steep banks on both sides, and so narrow that it is almost impossible to walk alongside of the cattle for any distance without leaning against them. The emigrants cut down a small tree about ten inches in diameter and about forty feet long, and the more limbs it has on the better. This tree they fasten to the rear axle with chains or ropes, top end foremost, making an excellent brake."

If the improvised brake, together with poles thrust through the spokes to rough-lock the wagon wheels, and the rope wound around a tree trunk all held, the perilous descent was a success. But if anything failed, then the oxen, the wagon and its contents tumbled downhill to end up as a catastrophic mass of animal flesh and debris.

Pioneer men and women such as these were among the first whites to penetrate the full breadth of the Cascades, and to see and ultimately define the features of this incredible wilderness. Along with their explorer predecessors, they dared, and sometimes even drowned in, its treacherous, tumultuous rivers. They gazed with awe upon its heroic trees; toiled up and skidded down its seemingly endless waves of volcanic ridges; encountered snows of a depth—30 feet and more—that not even their nightmares had suggested. They ferreted out its few passes; and, once arrived in the promised land beyond, they made peace with—or were killed by—its unpredictable Indians.

Their journey of discovery was a day-after-day, life-and-death struggle over a thousand mountains and a thousand cliffs, through forests that stretched farther than a man could see. To me, the persistence and daring of these people is a matter of special wonder—and pride: my own grandmother, Laura Ann Parsons Phippen White, a tough, doughty pioneer herself, traveled 2,000 miles from Wheeling, West Virginia, into the West aboard a covered wagon.

Though the Cascade wilderness was a formidable adversary, these mountains also unfolded the reward of their magnificent physical beauty. For a young New England writer named Theodore Winthrop, whose journal, *The Canoe and the Saddle,* became part of the lore of the Cascades, even the worst mountain passages were filled with almost mystic revelations. The following excerpt, derived from his description of crossing the Naches Pass in 1853, is typical of those impressions: "I had been following for many hours the blind path, harsh, darksome, and utterly lonely. At last, as I stormed a ragged crest, gaining a height that overtopped the first, I looked somewhat wearily across the solemn surges of forest. Suddenly above their sombre green appeared Mount Tacoma. No foot of man had ever trampled those pure snows. It was a virginal mountain, distant from the possibility of human approach. Only the thought of eternal peace arose from this heaven-upbearing monument and filled the world with deep and holy calm."

Winthrop had laid eyes on that monarch of the Cascade peaks, Mount Rainier—then called Tacoma.

Today much of the Cascades remains the same as when these early whites set foot there. The dangerous lower waters of the Columbia River, where members of many emigrant families drowned almost within sight of their ultimate goal, now lie submerged behind dams. But most of the mountain range itself looks the way it did centuries ago—a spectacular kaleidoscope of wilderness terrain. According to Bates McKee, professor of geology at the University of Washington, this part of the world contains some of "the highest mountains on the continent. The deepest canyons. The greatest concentration of active faults and earthquakes. The fastest ups and downs. . . . Virtually all the volcanoes; the glaciers. The most vigorous rivers. The fastest erosion rates. The greatest climatic variation. . . . The densest rain forests. The most devastating landslides."

The very first American citizen to tentatively probe the Cascades arrived by sea, on the Pacific Coast—and promptly discovered one of the range's dominant natural features. In 1792, Captain Robert Gray, searching for the huge mysterious "River of the West" he had heard about, sailed his sloop *Columbia* through the roiling water at the mouth of a great river and dropped anchor inside its estuary. Gray, whose voyage was sponsored by a group of Boston merchants, was surprised when "vast numbers of natives came alongside," but they seemed curious and friendly, watching the ship "with great astonishment."

Gray sent his crew 35 miles upstream to search for otter skins, barely far enough to encounter a barrier of fearsome rapids and gorges. There the crew came upon more Indians, but they did not find any otters. Disappointed, Gray sailed off after a week. Before he left, however, he claimed the river and all its drainage system for the United States —having no notion that this river rose 1,200 miles away in the interior mountains of Canada. Since he had already bestowed the names of his backers and contemporary politicians on other landmarks he had discovered up and down the coast, Gray named the river after his ship —Columbia's River—a designation that fur traders abbreviated to the Columbia a few decades later.

Thirteen years after Gray's voyage, Meriwether Lewis and William Clark, heading west from Saint Louis with their Corps of Discovery in 1805, encountered the Columbia just above the present Washington-Oregon border, where the river ends its southerly journey and makes a great swing westward through the Cascades and toward the sea. They tried to ride the river in dugout canoes, shooting through rapids, as their journals noted, with water "boiling and whorling in every direction." But the violence of the Columbia often forced even these intrepid explorers to haul out their canoes and portage. Of one climactic pitch of white water, they wrote: "This great river is compressed within the space of 150 paces in which there is a great number of both large and small rocks, water passing with great velocity foaming & boiling in a most horrible manner, with a fall at about 20 feet." Below the great falls of the Columbia, friendly Indians told the explorers that warlike tribes planned to massacre them—but the expedition was not attacked.

As they battled their way downstream, Lewis and Clark described the mountains on either side as "high, rugged, and thickly covered with timber, chiefly of the pine species." At one point they were much struck by "a very high mountain covered with snow, and from its direction and appearance we supposed it to be the Mount St. Helens"—which indeed it was, having been first seen from the sea 13 years earlier and named by the British explorer George Vancouver. "There was also another mountain of a conical form," Lewis and Clark added, "whose top is covered with snow, in a southwest direction." They were describing Mount Hood, the queen of the southern Cascade volcanoes as Mount Rainier is the king of the north.

The next discoverer of note to record his lasting impressions of the natural wonders of the Cascades was a young Scottish botanist named David Douglas. He came by ship from England in 1825, in behalf of the Royal Horticultural Society, to search the mountains for specimens. For a full year he wandered through the range, a pack on his back, a rifle over his shoulder, a shaggy terrier at his heels—and his wits very much about him. Early in his explorations, when Douglas ran into a dangerous-looking band of Indians, he pulled out a pocket lens and focused it to concentrate the sun's rays to light his pipe. The tribesman thought Douglas had used his power to call down fire from the heav-

As wild as the Columbia River was before it was dammed, this tributary, Oneonta Creek, runs down a gorge cut into 200 feet of basalt.

ens. And the story of this strong medicine must have spread quickly, for thereafter most of the Indians tended to leave him very much alone —although a few friendly ones helped him by acting as guides.

Climbing the western flank of the range, Douglas was astonished to find what he felt must surely be the greatest forests in the world. And they were very nearly that. Their dominant tree was a conifer growing 200 feet tall and more, with a diameter measuring up to 17 feet. With the sole exception of the then-undiscovered sequoias, this conifer was —and is—North America's biggest tree. Without exception it has since become the world's greatest single source of raw timber. In Douglas' time, these trees stood by the millions from tidewater right up to the edge of the glaciers, 7,000 feet and more above sea level, mantling hills and valleys like a thick layer of dark green velvet. The trees' thick crowns, joining high overhead, kept most of the forest floor in perpetual shade. Douglas had never seen anything like it. At first he thought the tree to be a species of pine, then guessed that it was a fir. The cones hung pendulously from drooping branches, and its twigs were wound with single needles. The brown, deeply corrugated bark on the trunk was as much as a foot and a half thick. Douglas stuffed cones, seeds, branches and bits of bark into his collecting bag, and sailed to England with this and 150 other "new" botanical species for the society.

Appropriately, the tree was named after him, and came to be known as a fir. Actually the Douglas is not a true fir *(Abies)* but is more akin to the hemlock *(Tsuga)*. Today it bears the scientific name *Pseudotsuga menziesii,* and the informal names yellow spruce and Oregon pine. By any name it has remained the lord of the northern forests. The vast stands of Douglas fir became the foundation of a lumber industry that was to attract almost as many emigrants, entrepreneurs and laborers into the area as the fertile plain to the west. Douglas, however, did not live to realize the importance of the tree that bears his name. On another expedition for the society in 1834, he fell into an animal-trapping pit in the Hawaiian Islands and was gored to death by a wild bull.

Only two years after Douglas' death, there arrived in the Cascades the first whites to settle and to leave a full chronicle of life in the wilderness. The very first wagon to reach the Cascades—in 1836—carried Marcus Whitman, a Presbyterian missionary, and his wife, Narcissa. (She was a special source of wonder to the Indians because of her long blond hair.) The wagon itself was a passion to Whitman, who, besides hoping to convert the natives, also wanted to prove that other families

This placid backwater in the Columbia River Gorge, bordered with sedges (foreground) and with maple, ash and willow trees (rear), shows one of the ways that damming has tamed the river. In predam days, torrential spring floods would have swept away the trees while they were still saplings.

could ride safely over the footpath called the Oregon Trail. His wife, however, failed to share this latter enthusiasm.

"One of the axle trees of the wagon broke today," Narcissa wrote in her diary one summer day as the party was on the east slope of the Cascades. "Was a little rejoiced, for we were in hopes they would leave it and have no more trouble with it. Our rejoicing was in vain however for they are making a cart of the hind wheels, intending to take it through in some shape or other."

In fact, the demiwagon did get across the mountains with the Whitmans—but not without some fearful effort, brought about by the unforeseen roughness of the Cascade terrain. As the party negotiated one series of typically tall and precipitous ridges, Narcissa wrote: "Before noon we began to descend one of the most terrible mountains for steepness and length I have yet seen. It was like winding stairs in its descent & in some places almost perpendicular. The horses appeared to dread the hill as much as we did. They would turn & wind in a zigzag manner all the way down. We had no sooner gained the foot of the mountain when another more steep and dreadful was before us."

But not even the toil and fear could blind the Whitmans to the beauty of the Cascades, and particularly to the drama of the same vista that had greeted Lewis and Clark 35 years before. "The sun was dipping his disk behind the western horizon," Narcissa wrote one evening. "Beyond the valley, we could see two distinct mountains, Mount Hood & Mount St. Helens. . . . Behind the former the sun was hiding part of his rays which gave us a more distinct view of this gigantic cone. The beauty of this extensive valley at this hour of twilight was enchanting & quite diverted my mind from the fatigue under which I was laboring."

Right behind the Whitmans, beginning in 1839 and continuing for almost 50 years, came the waves of pioneers. Their wagons—like my grandmother's—were overloaded with four-poster beds, dressers and stoves that they could not bear to leave behind. In the decades of their great migration the Oregon Trail became littered with such possessions, jettisoned as oxen grew thin and tired. The trail also became an elongated graveyard for about 30,000 men, women and children who did not survive the trip.

The wagon trains entered the Cascades near the present town of Walla Walla, and traced the Walla Walla River to the Columbia. Then they followed a tortuous path along the riverbank to a six-mile-long canyon known as the Dalles. The place was named by French fur trappers of the Hudson's Bay Company because its steep canyon walls reminded them of the stone-lined open sewers known by that name in their villages at home. The entrance to the Dalles was only 60 miles from the Willamette Valley, but that short passage frequently brought as much tragedy as the rest of the pioneers' 2,000-mile journey.

The cliffs of the Dalles rose too abruptly from the river to allow wagons to move along the water's edge. And though the ridges on either side of the river were almost impassably rough, some of the emigrants turned away from the Columbia Gorge at this point, abandoning their wagons and driving their livestock along single-file trappers' trails through the mountain defiles. To reach these dubious detours, the westbound pioneers and their livestock had first to raft or swim across the river, and in the process many cattle and some emigrants drowned. The majority of the settlers elected to try to ride the river downstream, shooting through the deep natural passage that the water had cut across the spine of the range. They disassembled their wagons, loaded families and possessions onto makeshift barges constructed from wagon parts, and pushed off into the Columbia. The Whitmans had come down to the river here, but prudently elected to portage around the rapids in the Dalles. Narcissa remarked on "two rocks of immense size & height, all the waters of the river passing between them, in a very narrow channel, & with great rapidity."

The lucky among the emigrants passed through on their roughhewn barges with the same rapidity, frightened out of their wits by the unfamiliarity of the surging water. But some unlucky ones drowned; and even more pioneers perished a few miles downstream at a fearsome stretch of white water called the Cascades—the place from which the entire mountain range derived its name.

Within a short time after the arrival of the first wagon trains, a group of enterprising frontier entrepreneurs had gravitated to the Dalles, where they offered to raft the pioneers down the Columbia for a price based on the size of their wagons. The emigrants, who usually had little money to spare, promptly named the boatmen the River Pirates —but often elected to ride with them anyway. One winter hundreds of emigrants, stranded at the Dalles, too poor to pay the River Pirates, too weak to try to struggle over the mountains, started to starve. They were saved only by a sudden charitable urge on the part of the Hudson's Bay Company's local boss, who sent several boatloads of food up the Columbia to sustain them.

By 1845, a Kentucky farmer named Sam Barlow decided there had to be a better way to cover those last 60 miles. Declaring that "God never made a mountain that he never made a way over it or around it," Barlow set out to find the way. With a party of hardy working hands, he began carving a track wide enough for wagons. Though Barlow himself was mounted, the expedition was short of horses: some of his men had to ride cows. Worse yet, winter set in while the men were still at work.

Nevertheless, in three months they managed to hack a trail through a notch at 5,000 feet between Mount Hood and Mount Wilson; they called their route the Barlow Road. It led westward—and precipitously—into the valley of the Zigzag River, and then down to the territorial capital of Oregon City. En route it plunged over the Chute on Laurel Hill.

Barlow was no philanthropist; he insisted on some compensation for his efforts and put a tollgate on his road at the trailhead. But he offered the emigrants a better bargain than they ever got from the River Pirates: no more than five dollars a wagon and 10 cents a head for loose animals, and no charge at all for a "widow woman" or a traveler who could not—or would not—pay.

On the day, 128 years later, when I climbed up the Chute on Sam Barlow's road, I stopped a mile above Laurel Hill at a peaceful little prairie called Summit Meadows, where many wagon trains had rested before descending. From there, Mount Hood looked close enough to reach out and touch. Indian paintbrush and dark blue gentian were blooming among tall green grass. A burial ground with weathered legends cut into stones marked where some travelers, infants and old ones, rest for good. I stared at the scene—headstones, flowers, mountains—thinking of the fortitude of the pioneers who came here through the wilderness.

Far north of the Oregon Trail, other emigrants kept probing for ways across the barrier—and discovering other features of the Cascades. Until a direct east-west route through the North Cascades was found, the more cautious and sensible pioneer families heading for Seattle reached Puget Sound by sailing boat from San Francisco, or overland through the central Cascades and then up the coast. But there were also the hard-headed ones who tried to batter their way straight across the northern mountains—which are even more fearsome than those along the Barlow Road. Entire wagon trains set off up the deceptively gentle slopes that rose out of the desert on the east side of the Cascades—and became lost, or blocked by cliffs too steep to descend, or stranded in snowdrifts too deep to escape.

Searching for a way across, one party of explorers turned back down

Mosses and ferns blanket boulders fallen from

a gorge near the Columbia River; eventually tree seedlings will find a foothold in soil formed by the decomposition of plants and rocks.

Douglas-fir trees, like these 200-foot giants, dominate the Cascades' western slopes in some places as high as 7,000 feet.

Whatcom Pass after their horses had starved, chest-deep in snow. Another train of 36 wagons, which had forded the Naches River in Washington 96 times, pressed on to the eastern summit of Naches Pass because the leaders had been told of a new road heading west from there. But there was no road, winter was settling in, and the pioneers seemed doomed. In an act of charity far exceeding even the food gifts of the Hudson's Bay Company, a crew of road builders on Puget Sound heard of the stranded wagon train and set out to rescue it. Hiking over the mountains, they found the caravan and then chopped a temporary path, foot by foot, back down the western slope. At times they had to kill oxen and twist the hides into ropes to lower the emigrants, their goods and animals down the cliffs.

In 1853, Isaac Stevens, the first governor of Washington Territory, sent one Captain George McClellan eastward to find a permanent land route that would allow emigrants to cross the northern mountains in comparative safety. McClellan (later to become commander of the Union Army in the Civil War) started for Snoqualmie Pass—at 3,004 feet the lowest notch through the Cascades. For years, coastal Indians had walked through the pass in summer to find berries and to trade with other Indians who lived on the eastern slope; Hudson's Bay fur trappers later used the same paths. Though the route looked feasible to McClellan in good weather, evidently he took the Indians' word that the annual snowfall in the pass (which subsequently was measured at 29 feet—and double that in the drifts) made a winter crossing impossible. For in due course he reported back to Governor Stevens that Snoqualmie was the wrong place.

Neither much impressed nor daunted by McClellan's report, Stevens sent another young officer, Lieutenant Abiel Tinkham, on the same quest a year later. With the help of a pocket compass and an Indian guide, Tinkham walked over the Snoqualmie in the middle of winter —and told the governor that a wagon road could indeed be built there. However, the territorial government had trouble raising money for the project, and the road was not completed for 14 years. When finally opened in 1868, it began for westbound emigrants at the Columbia near the confluence with the Snake River, cut through the pass and then led downhill to the new cities of Olympia, Tacoma and Seattle.

The Forest Service has preserved one twisting mile of the old Snoqualmie road just west of the crest. Walking what remains of the route not long ago, I was astonished that the pioneers had ever been able to

Leslie's weekly depicted the Modoc Indian surrender after the siege of the lava beds.

negotiate it. The trail is much narrower than a single lane of any modern road. The wagons had to squeeze around boulders and trees, and cross boggy stretches of forest floor covered with puncheons—split logs of cedar laid crosswise like bumpy corduroy. Like all the Cascade traces, however, the Snoqualmie Pass trail had its visual rewards. Near the crest the road passes within sight of Franklin Falls, where one fork of the Snoqualmie River plummets 85 feet into a graceful pool.

Down in the southern Cascades, westering emigrants found very different terrain—and different perils. Instead of cliffs and rapids, they were confronted by mile after mile of sere, barren lava beds—and hostile Indians. The Applegate Cutoff, named for two entrepreneur brothers, Lindsay and Jesse Applegate, was particularly notorious for the danger from Indians. It branched off the main California Trail in Nevada and wound past Tule Lake and Klamath Lake into southern Oregon. Along its route, the Modoc Indians ambushed wagon trains so often that one spot, where the road edged between Tule Lake on one side and a steep cliff on the other, became known as Bloody Point. In 1852, the Modoc massacred 64 of the 65 men, women and children in one emigrant train there.

Thereafter, through the 1850s and '60s, the Modoc and the pioneers sporadically murdered one another around Tule Lake and the barren expanse of igneous rock that has since become the Lava Beds National Monument. Hoping to end the bloodshed, the government tried to persuade the Modoc to move to the Klamath Reservation in southern Oregon. But the Modoc, who did not get along with the Klamath, held out for their own reservation in northern California. Finally, one dawn in November 1872, an Army battalion surprised the sleeping Modoc and ordered them to march to the Klamath Reservation. Instead, the Modoc—58 warriors and 102 women and children—fled to the lava beds and prepared for a battle. Their medicine man, Curly Headed Doctor, strung a red rope around their position; so long as it stayed in place, he said, all the Modoc inside would be safe. Their chief was Kientepoos (Of a Dark Color), who had been nicknamed Captain Jack by a local white judge. Captain Jack flew the tribal war flag—a mink skin with a hawk feather—over his cave.

About 350 soldiers, meanwhile, numbering some veterans of the Apache wars but also including some totally inexperienced troopers and volunteers, gathered about two miles away. Boasting that they would eat "Modoc steak" for dinner, they attacked across the lava beds in dense fog the morning of January 17, 1873. The Modoc, hidden behind rocks, picked them off one by one. After a fight that lasted until afternoon, the soldiers withdrew in confusion. They had lost 37 men, while not a single Modoc had been touched. That night many soldiers swore they would face 20 years in Leavenworth for desertion rather than attack the fortress again.

The Army sent reinforcements, including Brigadier General E. R. S. Canby, commander of the Department of the Columbia. After two months of minor skirmishing, leaders of both sides agreed to meet—unarmed—for peace talks in a tent midway between the lines. The night before the conference, Jack, under pressure from dissidents, agreed to kill Canby. The next day, in the middle of the peace talks, Jack jumped up, drew a pistol from under his blanket, aimed at Canby and pulled the trigger. The weapon misfired, but before Canby could react Jack pulled the trigger again and Canby fell dead with a bullet above his left eye. The Modoc also killed a white minister and wounded—and partially scalped—a white Indian Agency official attending the talks. Then they fled back to their redoubt.

Infuriated by this treachery, General William T. Sherman, Army Chief of Staff, ordered the soldiers to exterminate the Modoc. More reinforcements arrived, and they bombarded the lava beds with mortars. Five nights after Jack murdered Canby, a curious Modoc hacked at an unexploded mortar shell with his hatchet—and was blown to bits. He was the first Indian casualty.

The next morning the Army siege forces, more than 750 strong, attacked again; but the Modoc, fearing that their luck had broken, had slipped away in the night. Over the next few months the Army, with the help of renegade Indians, captured the Modoc, group by group. On June 1, they finally ran down Captain Jack, wearing Canby's tattered uniform, near Clear Lake. "Jack's legs gave out," said the captured chief.

After a perfunctory military trial, Jack and three other Modoc leaders were hanged at Fort Klamath, while the tribe watched in compulsory attendance. The Army then packed the remaining Modoc off to a reservation in Oklahoma, more than 1,000 miles from home, where in due course they succumbed to Sherman's wishes and became extinct.

One hot summer day not long ago, I ran my fingers over the juniper wood of Canby's Cross, which marks the spot where he died. A wooden sign with a legend carved out of the center tells all about the deadly incident. I have my own special reason for remembering the sign. A while back, vandals stole it and took it off to Susanville, 100 miles away, to use as a coffee-table top. The local police picked it up in a drug raid and turned it over to the Forest Service. On my way to Lava Beds I stopped off at the Lassen National Forest office in Susanville. And when one of the Forest Service people asked if I would return the stolen sign to the National Park Service, I decided I would lug it up to Lava Beds.

That night I saw a fire blazing near my campground. I headed for it, somewhat apprehensively. Recently, a forest fire started by lightning had swept through many acres of the area, turning the forbidding sage-and-juniper landscape as black as lava itself. But the blaze I had seen turned out to be only a campfire, where a ranger named Mike Quinn was telling half a dozen visitors about the Modoc War. I went back to my camp, got the heavy sign and took it to him. "I believe you've been missing this," I said. Then, by the wavering light of his fire, ranger Quinn read aloud to his guests the historic words inscribed on the marker from General Canby's Cross.

My son and I slept that night inside our station wagon, for we had heard there were rattlesnakes hereabouts that like nothing better than to slide into the warmth of a sleeping bag on the ground. Rising over us was a big juniper with dusty-blue berries, and through its branches winked the millions of stars of the Milky Way. Before dropping off to sleep I found myself wondering about the Modoc, the pioneers and my grandmother. I thought about everything those first settlers went through to reach this end of the continent—and I wondered if their descendants, if my own family, could face up to such a trek today.

NATURE WALK / Up Larch Mountain

PHOTOGRAPHS BY DAVID CAVAGNARO

Back when I lived in the Northwest and often traversed the Columbia River's flanks, I imagined scaling the beetling cliffs on the Oregon side of the river's gorge to see what lay beyond. I never did; few travelers do. Even those inveterate wilderness explorers, Lewis and Clark, merely marveled at the waterfalls that still leap from the forested heights and then floated on.

My chance came at last on a crisp late-October day. With photographer David Cavagnaro, I headed up the riverbank toward the 4,000-foot summit of Larch Mountain, a minor, extinct volcano misnamed by pioneers. Larches do grow elsewhere in the Cascades, but this mountain has none; the trees the settlers saw here were *Abies procera,* the noble fir. Our goal was only four crow-flight miles from the river but seven miles on foot through a diversity of geological and biological forms that local naturalists fondly refer to as "an ecological chaos."

Our trail began in the morning mists below Wahkeena Falls, one of a gaudy trio that includes Bridal Veil Falls and Multnomah Falls. Unlike its loftier and more ethereal neighbors, Wahkeena Falls is turbulent and pugnacious, roaring out of the cliffside to join the river below. Everything around it—ferns, bare rock, moss-covered basalt—is drenched in its spray. So were we, after climbing a series of switchbacks to the top of an escarpment 900 feet up the face of the gorge—and within earshot of Multnomah. Needing a breather, we hiked across to peer down the length of that delicate plume.

Far below, the Columbia glided by. Rudyard Kipling, steaming upstream here in 1889, asked the name of this waterfall. Bridal Veil, a crewman told him by mistake, and the author fumed. America already had plenty of Bridal Veil Falls, he said; and he evidently never did learn that the great "blown thread of white vapour" he so admired bore the majestic Indian name of Multnomah, after a tribe that once roamed here.

Kipling also described this stretch of the Columbia as "penned between gigantic stone walls crowned with the ruined bastions of Oriental palaces." The gorge does, indeed, present a façade reminiscent of classic Chinese painting: black basalt rock mantled in greenery, laced with plunging ribbons of water and boldly striped in brown horizontal layers, the eroded edges of old lava flows.

David and I, temporarily mesmerized by the ceaseless swish of falling water, were startled by a shape sweeping up past us from below—an osprey clutching a salmon in its talons. As we watched, the bird circled into the treetops overhead, seeking its nest, and disappeared.

We turned and entered a dark ravine carved into the hills by Mult-

A TANGLE OF VINE MAPLES

nomah Creek. Past a drippy, wet-smelling overhang of basaltic rock festooned with deer fern, we found another noisy cascade. A fallen tree was wedged into this spillway; one day the water would wear and wash it away. All around stood its neighbors, 200-foot Douglas firs. In the dim light at their feet, the understory of moss-hung vine maple was turning yellow at winter's approach.

A CASCADE OF WAHKEENA FALLS

MAPLE-GARLANDED DOUGLAS FIR IN THE LOWER FOREST

The morning was clear but with a lingering trace of the night's chill. Though the tips of a few of the tallest trees were already touched by golden morning light, the sun itself was still hidden behind the hills ahead. In this lower part of the forest many plants on the shaded north slopes never see the sun. Even in midwinter, when the maple leaves have fallen, the profusely needled evergreens shade the forest floor. Yet there is light enough for some plant life; in fact, within a few yards of the creek, where the canopy is a little less dense, plant life positively thrives. We saw clumps of sword fern spotted among ground-covering mosses and the bright green, triplet leaves of oxalis.

On Perdition Trail

We had now climbed above the basalt formations of the gorge and entered a region in which the underlying rock was shale. As we skirted the edge of the creek, David and I clung to abrasive handholds of this gray sedimentary rock, which once had been the bed of an ancient sea. It lay in hundreds of jagged, brittle sheets about a half-inch thick, all thrusting from the side of the ravine at the same 45° angle. Where the sheets had broken off, bits of shale sharp as glass littered the creek bed and slashed at our boots. This part of our route has been named Perdition Trail—possibly by someone who had traversed it barefoot.

Farther on, we passed through a short stretch of typical northern rain forest. Robust red alders reared among spindly vine maples and dogwoods beside Multnomah Creek. An occasional lacy-branched western red cedar, its bark thin and ribbony, appeared among the deeply corrugated boles of Douglas firs.

In this wilderness region of the Mount Hood National Forest, no logging is permitted. A tree toppled by age, disease or wind lies where it falls—a waste in the eyes of some loggers. Yet even in death it serves the forest's needs. Bugs and grubs and the processes of weathering break down its cellulose fibers for absorption into the soil. Grains of pollen, seeds and spores fall upon the log. Some of these seeds germinate and grow along its length, as in a nursery bed, free from the fierce fight for space in the crowded soil.

On one of these nurse logs a tiny, new bell-shaped mushroom with a creamy conical cap had sprouted only the night before. But already

MUSHROOM AMID HEMLOCK SEEDLINGS

it towered over a miniature forest of hemlock seedlings about an inch high. The most shade-tolerant of all conifers, the baby hemlocks were prospering in this dim light. Centuries from now, one or two might still survive, their roots having straddled the log and groped down into the rocky soil, while their crowns reached up as high as 150 feet.

Atop a larger mushroom on another log, a leopard slug was crawling —sluggishly, of course—its feelers and eyes reflecting the bluish morning light. On a third log, a fallen fir, a colony of shelflike bracket fungi was growing in a thicket of feather moss. The fungi may well have killed the tree while it was still standing, for this parasite has a threadlike and fatally poisonous filament called a hypha, which attacks and breaks down the tree's life-giving cambium layer just beneath the bark.

SLUG DESCENDING FROM A MUSHROOM CAP

BRACKET FUNGI ON A ROTTING LOG

CLUSTERED SNOWBERRIES

The minicascades along Multnomah Creek and the dozens of smaller streams that tumble into it have never been christened. I like to think of one of these nameless tributaries along the trail to Larch Mountain as "Sunny Creek." Here, at around 1,500 feet of altitude, the midmorning sun, poking at last over the ridges ahead, struck us head-on and illu-

mined all life along the stream. In no time we were sweating, and stripping off layers of outer clothing.

The sunlight fell on dangling white globules of snowberries, ready to drop at their season's end, and on the graceful fronds of sword fern, still green amid clusters of brown alder and canary-yellow maple leaves. It threw into silhouette the somewhat bedraggled webs of spiders. The webs had served their purposes as food-gathering storehouses and summer homes; now, like their occupants (which already had deposited their egg cocoons in nearby bushes), they were under sentence of destruction by the forthcoming storms of winter.

The sun also brightened the creek itself, and the moss-covered boulders, which the water had transported here, fairly glowed in shades of velvety green. These boulders were

slick as ice, as we discovered. At several points, the trail crosses Multnomah Creek. Anyone planning to cross it must hop precariously from boulder to boulder, erect or on all fours, clutching for balance at any stranded log that may be nearby. The logs are slippery too, being endlessly bathed in spray from the creek. I kept dry on every crossing but one. A perfectly solid-looking mossy rock tilted as I planted my boot on it and I was instantly in the water on all fours, up to the elbows and calves. I crawled out on the far side to rejoin David, who had skipped nimbly across—cameras cradled in his arms —without getting wet.

The Hemlock Mystery

The dominant tree in the forest around us was gradually changing —from arrow-straight Douglas fir to equally tall but droopy-topped western hemlock. I knew that the hem-

FRONDS OF SWORD FERN

A SUN-SPANGLED SPIDER WEB

A GLADE ON MULTNOMAH CREEK

lock is the climax tree of this region, thriving in shade and eventually elbowing out the more light-dependent fir. And I wondered why the hemlock here had not yet taken over completely. This train of thought led me to ponder an enigma of the entire Pacific Northwest forest.

DEER FERN AND MUSHROOMS

When white men in the 18th Century first laid eyes on these woods, an unbroken carpet of Douglas fir stretched for hundreds of miles along the Cascade foothills, running right down to tidewater. The trees were yards thick, and many were at least half a thousand years old. How, I wondered, had this enormous stand of firs—the greatest on all the earth —managed to stave off not only encroaching hemlocks but also cedars, spruces and other trees in the natural succession? Perhaps great conflagrations centuries earlier had opened the terrain to the light that Douglas-fir seedlings demand. No one has yet found an unchallengeable answer, and probably no one will ever know for sure.

In the hemlock forest we now had entered, at an elevation of some

A GROVE OF MASSIVE HEMLOCK

3,000 feet, the understory had vastly changed. Eight-foot skeletal stalks of devil's club, with sprigs of red berries among their clusters of maple-like leaves, stood at the feet of the big trees. The devil's club was not to be touched. The long yellowish spines that bristle on its stalk, and sparser barbs on the stems and on the undersides of the leaves can pierce skin like porcupine quills, and are as painful to remove. Somehow, deer and elk browse unscathed on devil's club, thorns and all, but I can think of nothing worse to chew.

Abounding Deer Fern

We had climbed above the range of sword fern, but the more delicate deer fern was everywhere on the ground, one clump with a spray of mushrooms growing like flower stamens from its heart. In front of another deer fern was a trillium, its lovely white flower now long gone, its three leaves brown and extensively chewed by caterpillars.

A few feet away, a garish little display of color caught our eyes. A single dark-blue berry of the clintonia, or queen's cup, hung next to a bevy of the bright-red fruits of bunchberry dogwood. Twice yearly the rosette of the bunchberry makes a gay punctuation mark on the ground: red in the fall and a blossoming of purest white in spring.

On a nearby decaying log was an odd sight—a slime mold's hundreds of spore cases aligned in rows like soldiers. The mold had been a mass of protoplasm oozing around and absorbing water and dead organic material, until some environmental

THE REMAINS OF A TRILLIUM

ROSETTE OF BUNCHBERRY

SLIME MOLD ON A FALLEN LOG

A GRASSY CORNER OF THE MARSH

change like a food shortage had made it dry up into spores. Now a puff of wind, a drop of rain or an insect's footfall could set the spores adrift like dust motes, finally to settle and start a new life cycle.

A Mountain Marsh

Off to our left we saw a clearing and we detoured downhill a couple of hundred feet to investigate. Here, in the first real elbow-space we had enjoyed since we began climbing out of the Columbia Gorge, David and I got our first view of Larch Mountain's knobby summit. But at the moment we were more intrigued by our immediate surroundings.

Our clearing was not man-made but a glacier-leveled marsh on a three-acre mountain shelf, a spot unmarked on any map and unlike any other along our route. In years of heavy precipitation the marsh might well become a shallow lake. But now, at the end of a dry summer and fall, it was an assemblage of small islands and ponds, hot and still in the noonday sun, though not malodorous like most swampy places.

This shelf and its marsh were hardly an ideal environment for the wind-blown or bird-dropped seed of conifers. And the trees showed it. Sparse, spindly firs, hemlocks and a few mountain ash were scattered among the drowned trunks of red cedar. With their roots in meltwater and lacking the nutrients abounding in forest soil, they were dwarfed compared to the grand specimens we had seen on our way.

Yet the place had a richness of life all its own. Sedges and marsh grass-

SPOTTED FROG ON A LOG

WATER STRIDER NEAR A STRAND OF SEDGE

FRUIT OF THE OREGON GRAPE

es grew thickly on the largest island, where birds must congregate almost as thickly in summer. The birds had flown now, but poised on the end of a log that jutted out from one island we saw a spotted frog, a Cascade denizen of wet places as high as 6,000 feet. It eyed us calmly as we approached, held still long enough to be photographed, then plopped softly into the water.

As the ripples subsided, we noticed another pond dweller, pouncing on a victim too small for us to identify. The diner was the common water strider, a familiar but always fascinating winged insect with three specialized pairs of legs. Feather-light, the strider moves over the film created by the surface tension of the water, rows with its middle legs, steers with its hindmost pair, and with its upraised forelegs grasps the tinier insects on which it feeds. Its body and the tips of its legs are covered with silken hairs that trap air to keep the creature from sinking if it accidentally becomes immersed. Mounted as if on pontoons and barely depressing the water's surface, the strider skims over ponds at high speed. The one we were watching paused near a curving strand of sedge, then suddenly took off and skated across the pond in pursuit of another victim.

Walking away from the pond, we paused on dry land to pick a cluster of Oregon grapes. The dusty blue berries, which had started life in springtime as sprays of brilliant yellow blossoms, tasted the way I remembered them: subtly sweet. (It is legal to pick the berries in this national forest, but all plants and blossoms are protected so that rare species will survive.) The leaves of this particular grape shrub had retained their lustrous green, though the early-fall chill had turned neighboring bushes a lovely dull red.

A CLIMACTIC STAND OF HEMLOCKS

Oregon grapes make a splendid jam, and when eaten off the bush, they color the lips and tongue as thoroughly as blueberries do. Blue-lipped, therefore, David and I ended our detour and climbed back to the trail to make our way, sweating, into the upper levels of the hemlock forest. We still had 1,000 feet of altitude to gain. And soon, through the trees and underbrush, we could see steep and rocky slopes ahead, past a point where the hemlocks came to an abrupt stop.

We emerged onto a steep slope littered with stones, and discovered the upper mountain to be covered with rockslides—the worst of which had wiped out the trees many centuries ago. Right ahead of us was a true talus slope, a rockpile at the base of a cliff. Elsewhere were other slopes composed of loose material, technically known as scree, that had slid downhill but without having first fallen off a cliff.

Pioneer Rock-Eaters

All the slopes were geologically interesting. The blue-gray rocks that covered them were not the basalt and shale we had encountered lower down. They were chunks of andesite, much younger, which had erupted from Larch—or from some earlier volcano—a million or more years ago. In some places among the fallen stones we found absolutely no signs of life. In others, only lichens grew. These are the pioneering alga-fungus organisms that, by exuding weak acids, disintegrate rock surfaces and, after centuries, help to begin the formation of soil.

Enough organic matter had drifted into still other areas of the slides to enable small plants to form a thin ground cover, like skin over a wound: fireweed, bear grass, huckleberry, serviceberry and gooseberry. In a few spots, the processes of soil building and of plant succession had gone a bit further, enabling some vine maples, mountain rhododendron and a few seedlings of Douglas fir to take root.

Between slide chutes there were even small trees that had been

FALL COLORS ON A TALUS SLOPE

spared for two or three decades. All their valiant struggles might easily go for naught. On any spring day, given the proper weight and temperature of a winter snowpack, a new slide of rock or snow might roar down to obliterate life, and force all the interrelated processes to start again from scratch.

We crossed the scree gingerly, walking on chunks of andesite precariously poised to slip away under any step. Not even lichen lived there, so far as we could tell. But on the far side of this scree we came upon a life zone of sorts. Scrubby vine maples and low-slung bushes of serviceberry struggled for a roothold, their leaves now mustard-colored and ready to drop at the hint of a fall wind. Fir seeds were twirling to earth in a gentle rain on all sides of us, from the thin forest of noble fir that we could see a few hundred feet above us, entrenched around Larch Mountain's summit. Still standing erect, in little clumps, were the stalks and already-mummified blossoms of pearly everlasting, the mountain flower that keeps its shape, blond color and structure long after it has died and dried out.

Some of these plants are marvels of adaptability. A few species, such as the vine maple, seemed rugged enough and flexible enough to grow anywhere from the green escarpment down at Columbia Gorge to this exposed and slide-swept mountainside. No matter how deep the shade, how thin the soil or how steep the slope—up to here, at least—the vine maple seemed unconquerable.

SUNLIT LEAVES OF SERVICEBERRY

A FALLEN FIR SEED

A TAPESTRY OF PEARLY EVERLASTING

Certain other species, it appeared, could survive only within the narrowest of ranges. An example of this was the dwarf juniper, a few specimens of which were clinging to the sheer rock face of Sherrard Point, a lookout just above us. Their home was windswept and dry—though it would be lashed by snowstorms in a few weeks—and it was exposed to malevolent extremes of temperature. Much more hospitable environments existed at lower altitudes. Yet it was only on that bleak promontory that we found the juniper, which evidently likes and prospers on the higher, bleaker, but sunnier ground.

We pressed on in the golden light of late afternoon. Thanks to our detour down to the swamp, we still had not reached Larch Mountain's summit. We were not losing enthusiasm; but we were getting tired.

The trail got steeper and rockier, and in the fading sun we got colder. Off to the left there was a much more challenging approach than ours, a cliff of bare rock that could be scaled only with pitons and ropes. We were not even tempted. We plunged on up the trail, not talking so as to save our breath. Rounding one turn, we saw a majestic sight that provided a double dividend for all the climbing and stumbling and foot-wetting we had endured. It was Mount Saint Helens, standing well to the north of the Washington bank of the Columbia. Its snowy cone was glowing as if the sun had set it on fire, and it seemed to light our way during those last steps upward.

We stood at last at the summit of

BEAR GRASS GONE TO SEED

rizon: Saint Helens, of course; then Adams and Rainier to the north; Mounts Hood and Jefferson to the south—all monarchical and snow-capped and the least of them more than twice the height of little Larch.

A gentle but penetrating wind wafted seeds away from the dead bear grass at our feet and tugged at the seeds of spidery fireweed, long since bereft of their magenta blossoms. Before the bear grass and the fireweed bloomed again, a dozen feet of snow would lie here, to remain until next May or June.

Westward, below a golden sunset, the Columbia flowed out of its gorge and on to meet the sea. The river had set its course millions of years before Larch Mountain was born and in all likelihood, it still would be running to the Pacific long after the mountain had worn away.

Larch Mountain, but hardly like monarchs of all we surveyed. Five massive Cascade volcanoes, rosy in the sinking sun, studded the hazy ho-

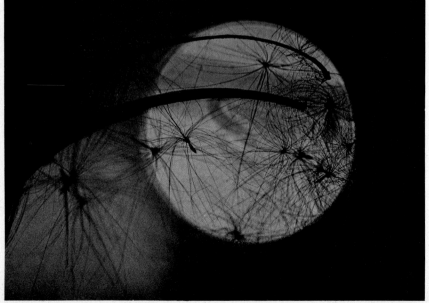

FIREWEED FLOSS IN THE SETTING SUN

THE COLUMBIA, WINDING WESTWARD TOWARD THE SUNSET

3/ White-cowled Priests

The whole mountain appeared as one glorious manifestation of divine power...glowing like a countenance with ineffable repose and beauty, before which we could only gaze in devout and lowly admiration. JOHN MUIR/ STEEP TRAILS

From Mount Baker in the north to Shasta and Lassen in the south, a strand of snow-crowned, dormant volcanoes rises far above the Cascade Range, like members of a white-cowled priesthood standing vigil over the world. And an imposing vigil it is. There are 18 of these distinctive volcanic cones in the Cascades, more than in any other range in the United States. One of them—Lassen in northern California—is the only volcano in the United States to erupt this century: from 1914 to 1917 it spewed forth mixtures of lava, mud and other debris 392 times. Nor are the other Cascade volcanoes dead; they, too, are only dozing and could awaken suddenly with enough destructive force to sweep away entire mountains—or the cities at their feet.

If one of the Cascade volcanoes were to let go tomorrow, its eruption —depending on the mixture of gas and molten matter in its deep earthen chamber—could burst out in a smothering deluge of light pumice pebbles, a lethal gas cloud several miles high, a luminous flow of brittle obsidian, or a great flood of molten basalt. This quiescent power is part of the fascination of these mountains. And yet, even without the lethal potential, their presence pervades the range.

From almost any point in the Cascades, at least one remote white cone lies on the horizon like an ambiguous tuft of cloud. And the face of each changes with distance and perspective. As you approach one of them it begins to take shape and then, as you round a forested hillside, the bulk of the mountain suddenly appears ahead, filling half the sky. Mount Rainier, the highest at 14,408 feet and grandest in the range, stands like a serene white palace, surrounded by flowered meadows; Mount Baker to the north is heavy, asymmetrical, imposing; Mount Hood in Oregon presents a cheerful, inviting, svelte form. Mount Shasta is a mystical, beautifully shaped dome; Mount Lassen appears dark and dangerous, seeming to bide its time before exploding into life again. Of all the Cascade volcanoes, Mount Saint Helens, a pristine mound of snow, looking neatly brushed in the morning, is my favorite.

Jim Ray, an old friend and mountain hand, suggested that we get a good night's sleep before we explored Mount Saint Helens in southern Washington. And we did. The woods around Jim's house were silent, without even the usual nocturnal scampering of small animals, only the faint ripple of a stream below the cabin. After having worked as a forest ranger for 40 years in the Cascades, Jim retired and built this place himself. He tried not to disturb the forest, and he succeeded. Black bears and mule deer come here in summer to feast on huckleberry leaves and fruit. Ptarmigans, the big grouse that change from brown plumage to white in the winter, come too.

In the morning I stepped out of the cabin to scoop water from the stream for coffee. There, looming through the firs, was Mount Saint Helens, bare and brown on the flanks, immaculately snowy on top, the most symmetrically rounded of all Cascade volcanoes.

After breakfast Jim and I hiked up a narrow trail that led above timberline over Windy Pass, on the east side of the volcano. Beyond the pass, a black valley, seemingly dead, spread out before us. Even though the plains lay below timberline, they were empty of trees; snow avalanches, channeled downhill within the confines of an old lava flow, recurrently flatten anything that grows in their path. A soft whirring made us look up, where a pair of ravens repeatedly swooped down to fight over something they had found to eat. A thousand feet above them the white cone of Mount Saint Helens brushed against the blue sky, 9,677 feet above sea level.

From where we stood in the pass, Saint Helens was not the only volcano in sight. Mount Rainier to the northeast, Mount Adams to the east and Mount Hood to the southeast poked above the fog.

Jim, a gentle man, began to speak with some sorrow of the paradoxical vulnerability of this massive mountain. "Saint Helens is one of the most fragile volcanoes of all," Jim pointed out. "This slope is deeply covered with pumice almost as fine as sand. Climbers and hikers come charging down every which way, ignoring the trails, and the pumice comes down right along with them. Look at all the shortcut trails around here; they're tearing Saint Helens apart."

He knelt to examine a plant. "There are only a few things that can hang onto such steep, soft slopes," Jim went on, "such as prostrate plants like this sulfur flower. And pussy paws, partridge foot, penstemon. Wherever one of them gets a chance to put its roots down, you have a couple of square feet of mountainside stabilized—at least until somebody's boot crushes it."

For the next two days, Jim guided me to some of the more spectacular vistas of Mount Saint Helens: we saw it mirrored in lakes, bracketed between slighter peaks, brooding behind soft veils of trees. Once we scouted it from a meadow on Mount Margaret, a few miles to the north. The meadow was a shelf on the mountainside: we stood two feet from the shelf's edge—and 2,000 dizzy feet above the base of a cliff. We scanned nearby ridges for mountain goats. Seven of them had been airlifted here from the Olympic Range in an effort to reestablish a herd that had died out years ago. But on this day the only movement we saw was a hiker working up a switchback trail on a far slope.

We climbed 100 feet or so to a crest of the ridge where two subalpine firs, with lilies blooming at their feet, framed Mount Saint Helens. On one side of the larger tree, six inches of bark had been clawed away, from four feet up the trunk down to the ground. "It looks like bear damage," Jim said. "They rake the bark to lick the cambium underneath, or to get bugs, or just to sharpen their claws. If they do a good enough job of it they kill the tree."

On a subsequent visit to Mount Saint Helens, Jim and I saw small herds of Roosevelt elk. Each herd consisted of an antlered bull, two or three cows and half a dozen calves, and they were browsing placidly. But then something startled one bull, and he and his family leaped downhill, their tawny rump patches wobbling as they ran.

The crown of Mount Saint Helens is smooth, too young to show the wrinkles of age—the ravages of glaciers, gravity and the weather. Though the mountain rests on the foundation of another, older volcano, the summit cone is the youngest in the Cascade Range, perhaps only 5,000 years of age. Like its near neighbors Rainier and Adams, Mount Saint Helens is a composite, or strato-, volcano built up by alternating eruptions of fluid lava and other material ranging in size from ash particles to blocks of rock as big as trucks, all tossed out of the crater at a velocity of hundreds of feet a second. During one eruption in

1200 B.C., clouds of ash from Mount Saint Helens floated as far as the present town of Banff, Alberta, 500 miles away. In another, in 1842, rivers of lava flowed as far as the Columbia, 60 miles off. One amazed witness to that eruption, a French-Canadian voyageur, noted that "the light from the burning volcano at my cabin 20 miles away was so intense that one could see to pick up a pin in the grass at midnight."

In another upheaval in the 17th Century, debris from Mount Saint Helens blocked the lower end of a large forested valley beyond the mountain's northern flank. Eventually the valley filled with water to become Spirit Lake. Skeletal trunks of 120-foot-tall trees still stand erect on its bottom. The local Indians stayed clear of Spirit Lake. Legend has it that a canoeload of Indian fishermen once drowned there when a sudden storm capsized their craft, and strange moaning sounds (actually produced by air currents) still echo across the water. Jim Ray and I crisscrossed Spirit Lake in a small boat owned by an octogenarian, improbably named Harry Truman, who has run a lodge in the shadow of Mount Saint Helens for 45 years. When Harry stopped rowing I thought I heard the low moans of wind song, too.

A Cascade volcano does not require a major eruption in order to become a colossal engine of destruction. In fact, a minor eruption from a crater or from a mountainside fissure may set in motion a glowing-hot avalanche known as a nuée ardente (burning cloud), which carries incandescent rock debris, and clouds of gas and dust many miles downslope. A nuée often travels on a trapped cushion of air; unimpeded by friction with the ground, it may move as fast as 100 miles an hour. A slight earth tremor, an abortive rumbling inside a crater, or simply an accumulation of rain or snow may trigger a lahar, the Indonesian word for a massive mudflow that can sweep down a valley in a flood of rock, mud, water and trees hundreds of feet deep.

Mount Rainier has discharged the most terrible lahars in the Cascades. The worst of all, which occurred 5,700 years ago according to radiocarbon dating of bits of wood it transported, has been given the homely name of the Osceola mudflow. It probably began at the top of Rainier, where steam and heat had gradually reduced much of the rock to a viscous clay. The whole mass suddenly gave way to the northeast and started downhill, gathering momentum and debris.

At 9,700 feet, the avalanche overwhelmed Steamboat Prow, a sturdy promontory that still bears clay-and-silt traces of the lahar; then it spilled into the streams that rushed down the White River and West

Fork valleys. Forty miles downstream the reunited flow, now 450 feet deep, curved west and poured out onto the Puget Sound lowland to bury some 100 square miles under at least 2.6 billion cubic yards of rock, silt, trees and mud. When it was over, the face of Rainier and the landscape around it had been totally reshaped.

Such destruction could happen again, on Rainier or any Cascade volcano that chances to be overburdened with winter snowpack and then drenched with a warm spring rain. If the lahar came from Rainier, a million people might be in the path of destruction, depending on the size and speed of the mudflow. The gravelly traces of one ancient lahar have been found under a garbage dump a few miles south of Seattle, 55 miles from Rainier. In case of a recurrence, perhaps half the city could drown in mud, for there would be no warning from the mountain.

The most recent lahar on Rainier occurred in 1947, only a few miles from the Osceola. This one devastated another valley that still looks as if the torrent had swept past only yesterday. After days of heavy rain, the lower mile and a half of Kautz Glacier on the south side of the mountain became waterlogged and broke loose, heading south down Kautz Creek. By the time the resulting mudflow overran the main highway into Mount Rainier National Park, four miles away, it was carrying 50 million cubic yards of debris, including boulders 13 feet in diameter. Mud-borne sand and glacial till rasped against trees along the creek and quickly cut them down. Those that were spared the initial violence died standing, smothered by debris several feet up their trunks.

Today the valley, its creek still eating away at the remains of the mudflow, offers a case study of how a slaughtered forest community can be reborn. In the spring of 1948, lichens and mosses moved in as pioneers upon the lifeless scene, attaching themselves to rocks, tree stumps and muddy soil. Next, wind-borne red-alder and cottonwood seeds lodged in the protected sides of rocks or rotting logs, and some survived. The alders were valuable in the birth of a new forest: their roots have the ability to take nitrogen from the air and fix it in the soil, so that other trees may grow. Bark beetles and other insects went to work, abetting the weather in decomposing the logs. Squirrels came to gather seeds; woodpeckers moved in on the insects; and hawks and owls arrived to live off the rodents. After a few years, Douglas firs began to crowd out the alders—and hemlocks began to grow under the firs. In time, the shade-tolerant hemlocks, the climax growth here, will inherit the earth around Kautz Creek—until another lahar buries the valley.

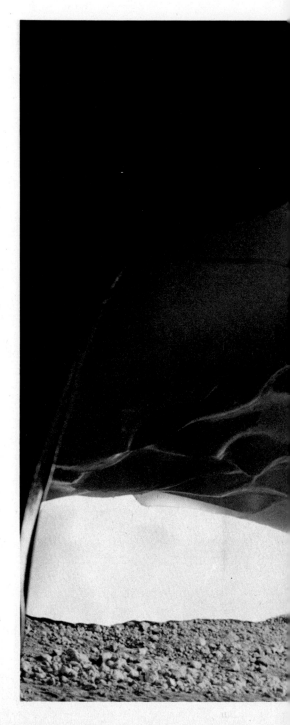

Sunlight, turned a soft blue, filters through the roof of an ice cave, carved by warm air currents, at the foot of a Mount Rainier glacier.

One recent day, my son David and I explored a stretch of the Osceola mudflow's pell-mell route through the White River Valley. Our path led up along the steep lateral moraine of Emmons Glacier, the largest glacier in the lower 48 states. The glacier lay on our left, S-curving out of sight up ahead, its broad surface littered with dead branches and the stony debris from recent rockfalls, and its interior showing sky blue where blocks of ice had broken off.

The milky headwaters of the White River tumbled out from under the glacier's snout. To our right an evergreen forest edged as close as it dared to the brink of the moraine; a bald eagle cruised over the treetops. The snowy upper slope of Mount Rainier, at the glacier's head, towered above us for a time, then vanished behind a thick cloud.

Abruptly a heavy rain began to fall, and we turned back. Far below, we crossed the White River on a teetering footlog and heard a rumbling that was different from the steady roar of cascading water and the pelting rain. It was the sound of stones bouncing over stones as the river nudged them downhill, a sound such as another Osceola mudflow might make. We got out of there.

A day later we walked up the opposite side of Rainier to the heights above Paradise Valley. The day was sunny, and spires of Indian basketgrass, or bear grass, were blooming into pale yellow pompons in the meadows near blue patches of lupine and bright, flame-colored splashes of Indian paintbrush. Dave and I climbed a snowbank near Paradise Glacier, and turned our backs to the mountain and saw 6,562-foot-high Pinnacle Peak, and the other black and rugged ramparts of the Tatoosh Range, below us across the valley. We descended a seldom-used trail along a narrow hogback and, as we passed a thicket of stunted hemlock, we were startled by a thrashing-about in the lower branches. A blue grouse, plump as a setting hen, emerged to stare at us for a couple of seconds, then fluttered back into hiding.

From Paradise Valley or its glacier you cannot see Columbia Crest, the true summit of Rainier, because a volcanic crater rim is in the way. There are two tilted, overlapping, saucer-shaped craters at the top; both are relatively new and uneroded. Under the icecap that covers the summit lies a remarkable network of tunnels and caves, melted out by steam from the volcano. These caverns, and a small hidden lake into which they drain, have been fully explored only recently, though for more than a century climbers have taken refuge there from storms.

Among the few to probe the depths was the ubiquitous naturalist John Muir, who noted "a sickening smell" when he sniffed the sulfurous fumes from steam vents on top of Rainier in 1888. A party of geological surveyors scaled the mountain in 1896, and were astonished to see hummingbirds streaking up Emmons Glacier, wheeling around the icy slopes and darting back down Winthrop Glacier. After spending the night in one of the caves near the summit, a member of the party named Israel Russell wrote:

"The cavern . . . was about 60 feet long by 40 wide, and had an arched ceiling some 20 feet high. The snow had been melted out from beneath, leaving a roof so thin that a diffused blue light penetrated the chamber. The floor sloped steeply, and on the side toward the center of the crater there was a narrow space between the rocks and the descending roof which led to unexplored depths."

The platoons of scientists and naturalists who have studied Rainier more recently cannot predict when this elegant giant will suddenly let loose one of the terrible instruments from its destructive arsenal. Snow avalanches and rockfalls drop off its honeycombed, steaming summit in every direction almost every day. And its soft, wet snowpack, with melting glaciers beneath, holds the constant threat of triggering a new lahar. Still more ominous is the possibility not only of a fresh volcanic eruption but also of a real cataclysm. Some geologists, including Professor Howard Coombs of the University of Washington, believe that Rainier could conceivably erupt at any time. The volcano is at a stage of geologic maturity when it could heave a great sigh of pumice and self-destruct. "Nobody can prove it," says Coombs, "but Rainier could devastate Tacoma and Seattle, just as Hood could destroy Portland." Other geologists keep warning that whenever serious seismic tremors signal a major eruption anywhere along the Cascades, all dams below the range should be emptied immediately to slow down the torrents of water and mud that might rush toward the cities.

I forget the reason for my first visit to Mount Hood, which is just as dramatic a landmark to the citizens of Portland as Rainier is to those of Seattle. I do remember, however, sitting in the vaulted lobby of Timberline Lodge on the south slope of the mountain and hearing the radio newscaster in London tell of the invasion of Poland by German tanks and planes. Snug in the lobby, warmed by the great fireplace, I doubt that any of us there dwelt for long on what had just been set in motion by the start of the Second World War.

I spent another weekend at Timberline last year, sleeping in the bedroom that Franklin D. Roosevelt occupied when he came to dedicate

Shrubs cling tenuously to Lava Butte, the cone of a volcano that spread lava over 6,117 Oregon acres some 2,000 years ago.

the lodge in 1937. F.D.R. declared the place to be "a monument to the skills and faithful performance" of people on the rolls of the Works Progress Administration. And monumental it is, a structure like no other in any American wilderness. Every massive beam and stone, every stick of furniture, every rug and painting and doorknob at Timberline Lodge was fashioned by human hands. The lodge was worth many times its $800,000 cost when it opened, and it has appreciated in value like fine wine ever since.

I slept well in F.D.R.'s bed, and in the morning went up the mountain with Annabelle Garcia, the ranger at the lodge. Because of a light snow-pack the previous winter, Mount Hood was naked beneath us. The slope, as we ascended, was covered by a layer of pumice, strewn with rocks that had bounced down from the summit crags. A few wind-dwarfed mountain hemlocks and subalpine firs had gained a roothold, but above them there was only a scattering of prostrate plants—alpine lupine and aster, dwarf purple penstemon, partridge foot—all hanging on to the loose pumice for dear life.

Despite its benign and open appearance, Mount Hood has taken human lives: I recalled the story of one roped-together climbing party that slid down a cliff of hard ice after one of them had lost his footing. They fell sitting down and as they shot past another group near the brink of a cliff they gallantly waved farewell.

Annabelle and I walked a long way to the edge of a wide, deep and barren trough where White River Glacier sticks a tongue of ice down the mountain. The glacial trough, both a river valley and an avalanche chute, fanned out thousands of feet below us into a wide gray slash across the green forest. The pioneers' Barlow Trail once passed along here; now its traces lie buried deep under the mud. A little residue of snow clung to the headwall of White River Glacier's source, a cirque that has scalloped out the mountain near Crater Rock; and there was some snow on the summit. For the most part, Mount Hood, which looked so smoothly conical from Portland 50 miles away, appeared senile without its cosmetic wrinkle-covering of snow, showing all too frankly the emaciation wrought by erosion. I preferred to remember the mountain with its make-up on.

Shasta is a lonely mountain. The volcano has double domes—the lower one called Shastina—that stand against the northern California sky, more than 1,000 feet above the surrounding terrain. Together the cones are more massive than Rainier but, at 14,162 feet, not quite so tall. To some people, the mountain's overwhelming bulk, or perhaps just its loneliness, connotes something occult, and the communities at Shasta's base are hotbeds of cultism. Among these are the "I am" sect (who believe they can speak with immortals), and the Rosicrucians (who believe that a race from the lost continent of Lemuria, submerged under the Pacific, inhabits Shasta's twin tops). There are believers in little people on the mountain, in big-footed people and bell-ringing people—and many others. I have no idea whether a kindred concatenation of cultists inhabits the towns nestled under other volcanoes, but their presence at Shasta is a form of reverence, and I respect them for that.

For some reason Shasta was not "discovered" until 1827, when a fur trader named Peter Skene Ogden climbed halfway up and wrote in his diary, "I have named it Mount Sastise," after a local Indian tribe.

In the wake of Ogden's discovery, 19th Century loggers lost no time in slashing through the stands of fir, pine and incense cedar that once mantled Shasta's lower slopes. As early as 1885, John Muir was scandalized by their cutting, which left Shasta looking like a man whose hair had been cut by putting a bowl over his head. Muir campaigned to save the remainder as a national park, but he did not succeed.

Muir climbed the mountain at least twice—the first time to see what would happen if he exposed himself to the unremitting fury of a winter storm. He descended several thousand feet from the summit to below timberline and then holed in, with a plentiful supply of firewood at arm's length from his shelter.

"Presently the storm broke forth into full snowy bloom," he wrote later. "The wind swept past in hissing floods, grinding the snow into meal and sweeping down into the hollows in enormous drifts. . . . But my fire glowed bravely. Day after day the storm continued, piling snow on snow in weariless abundance." Once, a large flock of mountain sheep took shelter nearby, beside a clump of dwarf pines. After a week Muir left reluctantly, at the urging of a guide who struggled up to plead that he was endangering the lives of people who were preparing to brave the storm to rescue him.

The next year Muir returned to the top of Shasta to take barometric readings, and nearly lost his life in another storm. Coming down after being stranded two days at the summit, he found his trousers were frozen so stiff he could not bend them at the knee, and he had to wrap his sore feet in sacking to walk. For a long time afterward Muir was lame, and the frostbite he suffered bothered him the rest of his life.

I went a good way up Shasta with John Wilczynski, a Forest Service

The greatest volcanic upheaval in the recorded history of the continental United States began when Lassen Peak blew its top in 1914 (left), and continued erupting off and on for seven years. The 1915 photograph below shows the skeleton of a grove still called the Devastated Area, where red firs and ponderosa pines were killed by a blast of hot gas and lava fragments.

timber-management expert, to see what grows there. We passed miles of plantations where foresters have tried to get ponderosa and white pines to reclothe the slopes. One method they have used is to drag plows across logged-off land to clear a 12-foot-wide swath through the thick growth of manzanita and snowbrush so pine seedlings can get a start. The pine plantations are, to put it mildly, a long-range project; the trees can take 400 years to mature. Meanwhile, some environmentalists have dubbed such cleared strips "porcupine freeways," because hungry porcupines run back and forth in the troughs and devour the tender seedlings at will. Some pines were growing, but they were outnumbered by six-foot-tall stalks of sweet-smelling Shasta lilies.

A little higher, Wilczynski introduced me to the first Shasta red firs I had ever seen. Technically they are called *Abies magnifica shastensis,* a subspecies of the California red fir; their thick bark is dull red on the outside and crimson inside. The word *magnifica* suits them. They grow in perfect Christmas-tree shape to 150 feet and more; needles on the higher branches form lovely snowflake-crystal patterns. Because early loggers passed up the Shasta fir in favor of bigger, more accessible conifers, the tree has survived—and even thrived—to elevations of 7,000 feet, where hardier firs and whitebark pines begin to take over.

In my opinion the view from the heights of Shasta is as grand as any in the Cascade Range. To the south, three creeks converge in a long valley to start the Sacramento River on its way to the sea. Farther south, a line of 6,500-foot battlements called Castle Crags stick straight up out of the forest, their contorted façades showing erosive action that has scoured them for 200 million years. To the west, a dark, perfectly rounded satellite cone, an offspring of main volcanoes, rises to within 200 feet of the summit. John Muir named the satellite for himself; officials of the Southern Pacific Railroad, whose tracks detour around its base, changed the name to Black Butte.

Lassen Peak is down at the end of the line, where the igneous rocks of the Cascades poured out on top of the older granite of the Sierra. It is not a particularly attractive mountain, but it has some impressive geologic credentials. Lassen itself is a dome volcano, formed of lumpy lava that failed to spread out laterally. Within a radius of 10 miles, you can see every other kind of volcanic formation in the world: the composite, created by flows of lava alternating with layers of explosively ejected rocks; the shield, or Hawaiian, type, made up only of lava flows and gently rounded like a Roman shield; and the cinder cone, built up by repeated explosive eruptions whose fragments fall back to the ground.

In May 1914, Lassen stirred into life when a brief, smoky explosion opened a new crater. Throughout the next year the volcano spewed forth a series of eruptions climaxing on May 22, 1915, in a massive outburst that was visible for hundreds of miles. This was a classic eruption that floated a mushroom cloud 30,000 feet in the air, spilled entire rivers of lava and mud down the mountain's flanks, and tumbled house-sized boulders to the valley floor, so hot they could not be touched for a week. Lassen also emitted one lethal nuée ardente, a blast that toppled trees three miles away.

Between outbursts a young man named Lance Graham went up to the summit with two companions to see what was going on. Fortunately he lived to tell the tale: "Just as I turned to leave the crater's rim, there was a puff of blue smoke, followed by a tongue of red flame that resembled the discharge of an old fashioned cannon. . . . I started to pick my way down the mountain, but in a trice I was enveloped in a cloud of smoke, while a perfect hail of small volcanic bombs and cinders beat down upon me. Then I was struck by a stone about twice the size of my fist that felled me to the ground. . . . When the eruption was over and the atmosphere cleared, my companions made a search for me, finding me completely covered with ashes and cinders. They started to carry my supposed dead body down the mountain."

I suppose it is partly morbid fascination that still draws visitors to Lassen Volcanic National Park each summer. On any sunny day, hundreds of them take off from the 8,500-foot level and trudge single file up the trail to the top, 2,000 feet higher, to peer into the steamy crater. Down at the foot of the mountain a seismograph in a stone hut at Manzanita Lake presumably would give warning if a new eruption were imminent. At two ominous enclaves called Bumpass Hell and the Sulphur Works, however, nature has provided warning enough: the rocks are brightly painted by sulfur exuded from acrid, underground, boiling springs; they show that Lassen has not yet given up, but is only breathing hot and heavy between exertions. One day Mount Lassen, like the other Cascade volcanoes, may come to life again.

Profile of a Living Glacier

From the dormant craters at its wrinkled summit (*opposite*) to the river valleys fanning off from its base, almost the entire face of Mount Rainier has been etched by masses of glacial ice. In all, 26 active glaciers, more than on any other mountain in the United States outside Alaska, crawl down Rainier, spreading out in broad valleys and building ridges of debris across the surface.

The biggest of Rainier's glaciers —and, in fact, the largest ice river in the lower 48 states—is Emmons Glacier, sprawling in a curving diagonal across the lower center of the mountain, as seen in the aerial view opposite. Five miles long and averaging nearly a mile wide, Emmons is at many spots as deep as a 25-story skyscraper is tall. Throughout its course, Emmons presents a dramatic example of the birth and life of the alpine glaciers, which for hundreds of centuries have helped to shape the Cascade wilderness.

Although Rainier's glaciers were first formed perhaps a million years ago, repeated volcanic eruptions destroyed each newly formed glacier. Thus the present-day Emmons Glacier is no more than a few hundred years old. Like many alpine glaciers, Emmons thrives on massive amounts of snowfall, and Rainier, only 50 miles from Puget Sound, offers a natural home. Westerly winds carry water from the Pacific Ocean, depositing the moisture as masses of winter snow—up to 50 feet in a single season. When more snow falls in winter than melts in spring and summer, the accumulation packs down and compresses into layers of ice —adding weight to the glacier.

In this annual cycle, new snow builds onto the head of the glacier while compacted ice melts off, and even evaporates, at the lower portion. On Rainier, whose volcanic core still gives off considerable heat, the melting process is intensified. Meanwhile, as the compacting and melting process continues, gravity pulls the glacier down the mountainside. Until about 1960, Emmons was retreating; unusually heavy snowfalls in the next few years, however, caused Emmons' forceful downhill march to accelerate to a rate of 100 feet per year.

The following pages provide a revealing look at the power and beauty of Emmons on the march—from its birthplace in the snow and ice fields at Rainier's summit to its end at the White River, whose headwaters are largely fed by this massive glacier.

Viewed from directly above the volcano's craters, glaciers fan out from Mount Rainier's summit like the arms of an immense starfish. The largest glacier, Emmons, flows down from the cone and curves toward the lower right-hand corner of the picture.

A rock ridge splits the badly wrinkled tongue of Emmons Glacier.

Scars of a Tortuous Journey

As Emmons Glacier works its way down Rainier, it builds up tremendous strains and pressures, creating crevasses and ice blocks which continually change the face of the glacier. The first of these occurs at the point where the frozen mass breaks loose from the summit ice field. This initial break creates a tremendous gaping crevasse called a bergschrund. Gradually, the original bergschrund is squeezed closed by great pressure from new snow and ice coming down from above —then a new crack forms above it, as a fresh segment of the glacier starts its own movement downhill.

Below a bergschrund, a complex webbing of crevasses splits the surface of the glacier—scarred signals that Emmons is everywhere on the move in an irregular series of slippages that pull the ice apart. These crevasses are created when the glacier moves over irregularities on Rainier's slope, and when the faster-moving center of the glacier pulls away from its sides. The size of these crevasses varies from a few inches to as much as 50 feet in width and 100 feet in depth. Rarely do crevasses go deeper than 100 feet or so, since the tremendous pressure that far down in the ice river tends to close together all holes and cracks.

Dark lines of dirt that built up between snowfalls delineate the front edge of a towering ice cliff—the upper face of the glacier's bergschrund— left behind as Emmons moves downhill.

A gaping crevasse, 10 feet wide and plunging to a depth of perhaps 100 feet, lays open the forbidding interior of the glacier. A deep crack like this can be a fatal hazard for skiers and mountain climbers, particularly if it is hidden underneath a layer of snow.

Sharp outcroppings of rock tear at Emmons Glacier like the blades of a giant harrow breaking soil. At a maximum stress point, like the one at lower right, a maze of crevasses intersect to form ice blocks—often as large as a house—called seracs.

The Massive Shaping of a Mountainside

Had it not been carved by glaciers and their runoff, Mount Rainier would stand as a more symmetrical volcanic cone. Century after century, however, Emmons and its sister glaciers have eroded away the mountain's surface, a fairly soft composition of pumice, ash and lava, leaving it gouged and abraded. As Emmons and the other glaciers gradually move downhill, they tear fragments from the mountain's bedrock —and pick up and carry along even more debris from occasional avalanches and rockfalls.

Some of this debris works down to the bottom of the glacier, creating an efficient grinding surface as the ice mass scrapes downhill. Much of it, however, is carried deep inside the glacier, until exposed by melting along the sides or at the glacier's end. Still other masses of rock and debris are pushed ahead or shoved to the sides, eventually to accumulate and come to rest as ridges called moraines—like the lateral moraine in the lower center of this photograph. Near the end of the glacier's course *(far left)*, the melting process has continued so long that the icy face of the glacier is completely concealed under the residue of debris.

The brutal advance of Emmons Glacier to the left of the ridge has inundated plant life and gouged out a broad valley. An older glaciated valley to the right has a sharper, V-shaped profile, and has become reforested with a new, relatively thick cover of conifers.

At the lower end of Emmons Glacier, a
large chunk of ice has broken off.
It lies amid layers of compacted snow,
ice and debris that the glacier swept
downhill. Just before this photograph
was taken, a light snowfall partly
covered the jumble of broken rock that
is characteristic of a glacier's terminus.

Below the glacier's end, meltwater,
milky with minute debris called glacier
flour, rushes through the stones of
Emmons' terminal moraine. Unlike a
rainfed river, which reaches its highest
point in the spring, a glacier-born
stream swells as summer heat greatly
increases the amount of meltwater.

In the last phase of its evolution, Emmons Glacier dissolves in watery runoff to feed the White River. Seen here along a riverbed, braided and dirtied with debris, the glacier rises to the right, toward its icy birthplace.

4/ A Garland of Waters

There I found five or six most beautiful small lakes grouped in a wonderful little glacial valley all ringed round with alpine larch. From the highest up, over an entrancing fall tumbled the water from a small glacier. A. H. SYLVESTER

It was just starting to get dark on a summer evening in 1853, and John Wesley Hillman, a young prospector, was riding through a peaceful forest some 7,000 feet up in the mountains of the southwestern Oregon Territory. No other white man had come this way before. Hillman was tired, dozing in the saddle and letting his horse find its own trail. Suddenly the animal stopped, stiff-legged, and Hillman came to with a start. Only a step ahead, a precipice dropped straight down more than 1,000 feet into a deep blue lake.

Hillman gingerly backed his horse away from the brink and then took an astonished look—the first glimpse ever recorded by a white man —at Crater Lake, round as a wheel, completely encompassed by vertical cliffs, and since judged by a fair number of people to be the most beautiful lake in the entire world. I would go further and call it the most beautiful lake in the entire Cascades—a praise I consider to be at once more specific and higher.

Throughout these mountains lie more than 1,000 other patches of water that carry the title of lake. In the 30 short miles of geological chaos between Snoqualmie and Stevens Pass there are no less than 692 lakes; south of Snoqualmie, in the 200 miles down to the Columbia River, the Cascades Crest Trail passes 260 more. The largest is a 55-mile-long finger lake named Lake Chelan, which heads a spectacular arctic cleft of rock walls and ends in a temperate plain of apple orchards. The smallest is some one of the nameless puddles that dot the al- pine meadows. And in between are hundreds of glacial tarns of all sizes, steep-banked mountain pools that were scooped out long ago by the earth-moving force of glaciers. They nestle high in the folds of the mountains, fed by snow, frozen in winter, ice-cold in summer.

There are, in all, too many of these lakes for any one person to know them well. Of the two dozen or so I do know, I have certain favorites —some that I have known for most of my life and others that I have dis- covered only recently.

One is Crater Lake, which fascinates me as it fascinates just about anyone who looks upon it, shimmering inside the vast, collapsed cone of a volcano called Mazama. In its prime, Mazama was probably 12,000 feet high. Snow-capped, glacier-clad and intermittently active, Maza- ma lived for hundreds of thousands of years and its death throes 6,600 years ago must have been awesome to behold. Human beings wit- nessed the sight: Indian tools made out of obsidian and fragments of basketry have been found amid the rubble of Mazama's heroic last gasp. What the Indians saw—and may not have escaped—was the self- destruction of a fire-mountain erupting clouds of pumice-bearing steam that drifted for hundreds of miles.

The fallout of Mazama's featherweight pumice still coats every sin- gle mountainside and valley in the entire Pacific Northwest. On the Pumice Desert northwest of Crater Lake, the blanket of fallout is some 50 feet deep, and scientists have determined that an inch or two still lies on the ground 600 miles away in southern Saskatchewan. For several years following these vast exhalations of dust, there were in- tensifications of dramatic color in sunrises and sunsets, as the light was refracted by the microscopic particles of Mazama's pumice hang- ing suspended in the stratosphere.

In its final hours Mazama also overflowed with glowing torrents of lava that coursed down its glacial troughs, snapping off trees and turn- ing the valleys into rivers of molten rock. Finally, all that remained of the original volcanic mountain was a fragile, hollow shell—which sud- denly collapsed. When the cataclysm ended, some 15 cubic miles of mountaintop had simply disappeared. The question of what happened to all that mountain puzzled geologists from the time of the lake's dis- covery until 1942, when California scientist Howel Williams published what is considered the definitive study on the formation of the basin. The greatest amount of blown-out material that Williams' research could account for, including ashfalls, lava bombs and molten avalanches, was 10 cubic miles. Williams finally concluded that five cubic miles of Mazama had simply been gulped down, collapsing back into magma chambers under the volcano.

Mazama's shell took centuries to cool; meanwhile, in the crater a lake began to form, fed by a few springs seeping through the buried debris of an old glacier. Snow and rain further nourished the lake, eventually filling it even beyond the present depth of 1,932 feet; traces of diatoms, single-celled aquatic organisms, still exist 50 feet above today's shoreline. During the 20th Century, however, the level has varied little, since the annual average precipitation of 69 inches has been balanced by evaporation and seepage.

While the lake was still building, a tiny volcano began to poke above the surface, spitting cinders until it had achieved a modest height of 763 feet above the level of the water. Today that minivolcano, now dormant, is known as Wizard Island, and stands like a model of the original Mazama. Wizard is separated from the lake's west shore by a narrow channel. I crossed it on a warm summer day with ranger Bruce Kaye.

When we landed, we could examine more closely the tall western hemlocks, a yard thick at their bases, that cover the shore of the little volcanic island. A fuzz of staghorn lichen marked each trunk down to a point 8 to 10 feet above the ground—the depth of the previous winter's snowpack. Below that the lichen, without light, had stopped growing.

Stepping over black blocks of lava, we found a trail that spiraled steeply toward the volcano's top. Near the base we walked through a belt of symmetrical Shasta red firs; they appeared to be thriving in this combination of volcanic soil and southern exposure. Farther uphill the ground covering of crumbled cinders, tinted brown and pink by iron oxide, supported only a few clumps of red-leaved Newberry's knotweed. The summit was encircled like a crown of thorns by silver-gray whitebark pines, seeming to be half-dead, most of them dwarfed by centuries of wind. These are doughty, admirable trees, a species that can cling to life at higher altitudes than any other in the Cascades because the virtually moistureproof bark, stubby needles and low-lying, pliable structure of the trunk and branches have all evolved in resistance to the cold and drying winds.

The rim of Wizard's crater, 400 feet wide and 90 feet deep, was surrounded by such pine trees. Inside the rim, two cocky, flashy-blue Steller's jays and a small furry creature known as a pika were scuttling about looking for seeds. The pika's cry of alarm has been described as

Crater Lake's Wizard Island, a minivolcano within a volcano, glows in a February dawn against the backdrop of the crater's lofty rim.

a nasal *eenk*, and that was exactly the sound this one made when it saw us. It was dark, about half the size of a grown rabbit (to which it is related), and had small rounded ears, a short tail, and fur padding on its feet to help it leap from rock to rock without losing its footing. The pika lived somewhere in the crater's litter of lava blocks, where it was accumulating stores of food for winter. Besides nourishing the pikas through the cold months, these caches of seeds and dried grass become tiny underground nurseries for trees. The uneaten seeds sprout, sending roots deep into the lava, eventually breaking down the rock, and building humus from their own needles.

Except for the pika and the jays, Bruce Kaye and I were alone on top of Wizard, which must be one of the United States' more private places. From where we stood, the world seemed virtually to end at the rim of Crater Lake, with only Mount Scott, off to the east, interrupting the skyline of the rim. Bruce pointed across the ring of pines to a red fir tree on the island. "A pair of bald eagles nested in that tree for years," he said. "They moved away, but if you're lucky you still can see bald eagles cruising around here now and then."

I remembered an ornithologist's field note I had once read: he had noticed some creature sculling along, far out on the surface of Crater Lake. When he focused his binoculars on it, he saw that it was an eagle, using its wings breaststroke fashion, and making fairly good time. Though we could not spot any eagles, half a dozen California gulls were flapping below us, snow-white dabs against the water. Crater Lake is far to the north of the High Sierra lakes where the gulls normally nest and breed, and these particular birds may have moved north looking for cooler weather.

Many other birds make Crater Lake a regular resting place or breeding ground. In the fall and spring, migrating Canada geese use the lake as a checkpoint, turning as they head to or from their refuge at Upper Klamath Lake, 30 miles to the southeast. In a single half hour one spring day, more than 5,000 of the big black-headed birds were counted as they flew northward, honking, across Crater Lake.

As we headed back down the corkscrew trail from the top of Wizard, I looked across Skell Channel, where the island's shore comes to within a few hundred feet of the steep rockslide at the lake's rim. Skell's water is bright green and shallow, covering a bed of lava flows. The channel is the natural route for any mainland animal—deer, porcupine, bear, chipmunk—that decides to swim out to the island for a visit. The animals often start rockslides along the way; all it takes to get a rockfall tumbling from the crater's rim is the weight of one squirrel, scampering across the top of a loose pumice slope.

In winter, Crater Lake is white-walled with snow. Yet its high, sheer walls, its broad expanse and the moderate climate keep the lake from freezing regularly. In fact, Crater has frozen over only once that anyone knows of—in 1949.

Back on the mainland Bruce Kaye and I started hiking the trail back up to the main crater's rim. Behind us the lake was a smooth mirror of light blue, glistening in the sun. But as we climbed, the water's hue seemed to shift—to violet, to Prussian blue, to steel blue, to indigo—as the light waned and the sun's angle changed. When last I looked, Crater Lake was a haunting, almost ominous, midnight blue, perhaps the color that led the startled prospector John Wesley Hillman to first name it Deep Blue Lake more than a century ago.

Later that summer, I traveled to a very different kind of lake, mile-high Hosmer near Bend, Oregon and adjacent to the Crane Prairie Reservoir. Hosmer is an adopted home of that fascinating predatory bird the osprey, a species of fishing hawk, which has become scarce in most of the country, and of schools of transplanted Atlantic salmon, which themselves have become scarce in their native habitat 3,000 miles to the east. My trip to Hosmer actually started quite by accident in a small public library at Mount Shasta, where I met a fellow browser who looks almost exactly like Carl Sandburg. He was George Matusek and he owned an insurance business at Dunsmuir, California. He was on his way to Bend in a few weeks, and asked if I would join him in his canoe and paddle around Hosmer Lake to watch the ospreys fishing for Atlantic salmon. I said that sounded fine, and a few weeks later we did manage to get together again.

Actually I had seen both the birds and the fish before—but not together in the same place: my first look at the slender-backed Atlantic salmon had been in June at the Wizard Falls fish hatchery on the Metolius River, where they have been raised successfully for 20 years. (The salmon are kind of a sideline at the Metolius hatchery; the hatchery's main business is breeding rainbow and brown trout.) After growing to 8 or 10 inches at the hatchery, the salmon are released by the Oregon Wildlife Game Commission in just a few landlocked lakes in the southern Cascades. As for the ospreys, I had seen them two months earlier at Crane Prairie Reservoir, an ideal refuge. The reservoir was formed by the damming of the Deschutes River; rising water

In July, retreating snowbanks still rim a nameless lake high in the north-central Cascades, where annual snowfalls may top 40 feet.

left thousands of lodgepole pines partially submerged along the banks. These trees are now a forest of dead snags where the big fishing hawks have built about 100 nests.

One day during this prior visit, while standing on the marshy ground at Crane Prairie, I held my field glasses on three ospreys gliding through the trees like bombers coming in for landings. When I turned away, I saw that a yearling mule deer a few yards away had been watching the birds too. Now it melted back into a dense pine thicket where squirrels and chipmunks had their own refuge, unmolested by hawks and eagles that would quickly catch them out in the open.

Right on schedule, I met George Matusek at a campground just beside Hosmer Lake. He had brought his canoe on top of his pickup truck, and I helped him carry it to the water. "Before you step in," he warned, "bear in mind that this is a white-water canoe, not designed for a lake. It will draw only two inches of water, even with both of us in it, and will be very tippy. No sudden motions, or over we'll go."

Paddling carefully through a curving inlet that leads to the main lake, we skirted thick patches of reeds and glided over hundreds of yards of water lilies. I gingerly reached out once to pick an aquatic plant, and managed to get it without dumping us into the water. During the day we saw only two other people, a teen-age boy and his father, fishing from a rowboat. They said they had had no luck with fishing, although the boy had glimpsed a family of river otters frolicking around a log. In the middle of the lake we stopped by a grassy island and just waited, sitting still, while afternoon shadows mounted the black cone of 9,000-foot-high Bachelor Butte a few miles to the east. The lake is shallow; the bottom at this point was only three feet beneath us, a sand-colored flooring of pumice where thousands of flies were hatching, crawling and floating to the surface.

"Know why I come here?" George asked. I said I supposed it was to fish; he had been tying flies and tapered leaders when I arrived. "No," he said, "not here. Basically I do love to fish—and you can fly-fish here for rainbow, brown trout and Atlantic salmon. Incidentally, there's a release law on the salmon. If you catch one you have to handle him tenderly and quickly ease him back into the water. Even in that little time in the air he gets confused; you have to give him a shove, right side up, so he can swim away. I really come here to watch the ospreys fish."

We waited a long time. Two ospreys took off from the tops of faraway pine trees, but they headed south toward their refuge at Crane

Prairie. George had time to tell me his life story: he had fled his native Czechoslovakia just before the Second World War, spent several years with the United Nations in Paris as a stateless-persons expert, and finally settled in California because it gave him such a wide choice of wilderness to wander. I told him of the time I had come across a young fellow trying to tend a wounded osprey on a bank of the Deschutes River below Sunriver. The bird had broken a wing diving for a fish, and the young naturalist was trying to soothe it so that he could get near it to give first aid. He finally managed to pick up the bird and took it home, but it died the next day.

As we talked, George told me more about ospreys: they have a wingspread of five or six feet, they usually mate for life, and they migrate to Central and South America for the winter, occasionally flying all the way to Brazil in 10 days. They return in pairs to the same nesting sites year after year, and each spring they produce one to four chicks, which, as they mature, grow white pantaloons like those of the bald eagle. Unlike most birds of prey, ospreys feed exclusively on fish. The male does the fishing and brings the catch back to the nest at least twice a day, eating the head of the fish himself and saving the choice body meat for his mate and chicks. The female then tears off one sliver of fish at a time, while each of the young—unlike most birds—waits patiently for its turn to be served its share from her beak.

After a while, a school of a dozen sleek gray-green Atlantic salmon, some nearly two feet long, passed near the canoe, moving fast. A few minutes later we heard a loud screeching and a big gray-and-white osprey, flapping along 100 feet overhead, suddenly hovered, retracted its wings and dived straight down. It hit the water feet first, making a splash as loud as that of a grown man doing a belly flop. As the spray fell back the bird took off triumphantly, shaking free of the water, a 10-inch fish clutched securely in its elongated talons.

We saw no more ospreys—and never did see any bald eagles, which often hijack the osprey's catch in midair. But we paddled past three more schools of Atlantic salmon on our way back to camp.

The father and son had left when we went by the spot where they had been fishing, but in the reeds a family of river otters, parents and two pups, their fur dripping wet and glistening, were playing follow-the-leader. They jumped off a half-submerged log, swam a few feet with whiskered faces held high and slithered back onto the log. They paid no attention to us until the canoe was a dozen feet away, then they flounced into the reeds and disappeared. Their coats were brown—not

Relaxed but vigilant, a yellow-bellied marmot sprawls on a sun-warmed rock. At the approach of any predator, the plump rodent emits a shrill whistle that warns its kind—and other alpine creatures—of the incipient peril.

the dark gray of sea otters—and they were in constant motion. River otters are beautifully streamlined creatures, and gorgeous swimmers, with long, tubular bodies and thick tapering tails. Their webbed hind feet have hard spikes to keep them from slipping on ice or underwater rocks. On land, they move in an awkward undulating weasel-like gait; in snow they swim along in a bellyslide, folding their forefeet back against their chest and using their rear feet as pushers.

By the time we got back to camp and pulled the canoe out of the water, the sun had gone down. I felt stiff and cold after hours of sitting nearly immobile on a kapok cushion. Paddling back had not been enough exercise to warm me up. George's wife Jan had a good fire going, but my hands shook and my teeth were chattering when she handed me a cup of coffee laced with bourbon. Even on a sunny August 26, the temperature at Hosmer Lake can drop from 80° to freezing, just after sundown.

The Green Lakes in Oregon's Three Sisters Wilderness are a few miles north of Hosmer Lake. The only way to reach them is by a narrow, crooked trail—a path I had been eager to follow ever since a friend named Towner Menefee told me that the lakes were isolated in a beautiful high-mountain setting that gave them a lonely appeal all their own. Towner is an energetic businessman in Bend, has seven children and, like many another hard-pressed householder, welcomes the excuse of an overnight camping trip to get away from it all. He is also an exceptional sportsman—a husky, tireless polo player and a good amateur pilot—but not exactly a professional when it comes to throwing a diamond hitch over a pack animal's load.

Because Towner is an avid equestrian, we decided to horsepack in to the Green Lakes, rather than hike and carry our own camping gear. Our route covered varied terrain, some of it steep and rocky and thickly forested, some of it grassy prairie. Our progress was, to say the least, a bit uncertain. On a barren slope about nine miles up the trail our pack horse, Skeeter, suddenly reared up and threw off his load, which, truth to tell, had not been snugged down as securely as it might have been. Fortunately the load fell uphill and just lay there (if it had gone downhill we might still be scrambling after it), so that we were able to repack Skeeter's load in a few minutes and get underway again.

The next thing to hit the ground was me. During our brief trip I had been sitting comfortably on an apparently gentle Appaloosa named Molly. She had held steady as a stone during Skeeter's shenanigans.

The first splashes of fall color tint a meadow, where tiny glacial tarns shimmer beneath the hulking whale-backed ridge of Crescent Mountain and the distant north face of Mount Rainier.

We had moved farther up the slope and were on perfectly level ground when all at once Molly unaccountably jumped sideways, quick as a cat, leaving me spread-eagled in midair like a sky diver. I came down on my palms and toes. After a moment's contemplation and inspection, I was surprised to find myself unhurt, and grabbed the reins as Molly circled in a nervous dance. Towner just watched, looking puzzled, as though Molly and I had done it on purpose. For all I know, that's just what Molly had in mind.

"Now what in the world was that?" Towner asked, and I shrugged. "Something spooked her," he said. "A bug, a rock in the trail, maybe she thought she saw a snake, who knows?"

Whatever it was, nothing else spooked Molly on the whole trip.

We rode out of the woods and up along a noisy stream hemmed in by a belt of subalpine fir on one side, and a towering, glinting wall of obsidian blocks that once had boiled out as lava from South Sister, which at 10,358 feet is the tallest of the Three Sisters volcanoes. At the top of this tight little valley I could see that the stream was the final outlet for the water from one of the three Green Lakes.

We paused to look around and let the horses rest. The Green Lakes, separated by banks of snow, lay in a long hollow scooped by an ancient glacier from the earth between South Sister and the neighboring Broken Top Mountain. At the near end of the hollow, snowbanks still ran down to the water's edge; at the far end, the last pond of quiet dark-blue water dissolved into marshy meadow, which gently sloped up to a stand of pine and fir. To our left ahead, a glacier on the east side of South Sister descended almost to the edge of the largest lake.

Suddenly, a high-pitched, hooting whistle came from somewhere in an obsidian flow on the rockslides above the water. Then we saw the source of the sound. Standing on a rock, silhouetted against the sunlight, a yellow-bellied marmot was watching us. I had seen Olympic marmots the year before, but never the yellow-bellied species. This one was two feet tall, yellowish across the chest, with tiny ears and an alert cock to its head. It whistled again, then ducked into the rocks. Its den would be deep within them, safe from such predators as wolverines, yet near the delicious grass edging the lake.

Towner and I decided to camp overnight on the dry and wooded east side of the main lake. To get there we had to cross deep ponds and wide snowbanks. We forded the ponds, feet held high out of the stirrups to stay dry, and plunged through the snowbanks, where the horses sank through the crust up to their knees.

We finally unpacked in a grove of mountain hemlock and tied the horses to trees 100 yards away. The afternoon was hot, the sun had not yet gone out of sight at the top of South Sister and we stood looking at the clear water a few feet below us. Towner said, "What about a fast dip?" We stripped, ran to an overhanging rock and dived in. Our bodies were shocked by the sudden cold, for the water seemed almost freezing. Twenty strokes out and 20 back were enough; we climbed out, whooping and hollering, and grabbed towels to dry off.

Long after our side of South Sister and all of the Green Lakes were in shadow, the sun still shone on Broken Top behind us. (Broken Top, another ancient volcano, is named for a great gash that has been eroded out of the south side of its cone.) The twilight was long and peaceful, and after our cooking fire died down, the night was so utterly silent that the gentle whinnying of the horses woke me twice. The moon was hidden. The lake became invisible and South Sister rose as a massive shadow, its pale snowy summit looming 4,000 feet above where we slept, blotting out the stars. Soon after daybreak I walked down to the shore to get a bucket of water. The surface of the lake was mirror-flat, reflecting South Sister in a pinto coloration of white and brown. I stepped with care because, in patches of grass and moss along the bank, hundreds of dwarfed Indian paintbrush were opening their maroon blossoms among the many deer tracks. Towner had been right about the Green Lakes. They were absolutely lovely, and I hoped the trail to them never would become too well worn.

After the night at Green Lakes, I knew my family would like this country west of Bend, and a few weeks later I took them to nearby Todd Lake. It is only a few air miles from the Green Lakes, South Sister and Broken Top, but rugged ridges lie between. At first, Todd Lake looked like no place for us; the near end was crowded with campers, trailers and hordes of shouting children. But we backpacked to the far end of the lake and found an isolated clearing where we could cook dinner and spread our sleeping bags in peace.

Even smaller than the Green Lakes, Todd Lake is placed at the bottom of a horseshoe-shaped amphitheater that rises like the curve of a 1,000-foot-high football stadium. The lower end of the lake is dammed by a moraine formed from debris the glacier left behind when it melted. The lake is now filling up and shrinking as silt runs down the banks and dying plants accumulate on the bottom. Ultimately most of the lake will become a moist mountain meadow.

A few Clark's nutcrackers—smoky-gray birds with spottings of white on their wings and tail feathers—looked on as we built a fire and cooked a stew, but they flew off at the intrusion of a dozen white-collared Canada jays. The jays darted among us, silent as bats, snatching crumbs and peanuts from the ground, even filching bits of food from our mess kits. When they had eaten their fill they left.

The jays, known as camp robbers, habitually outwit the nutcrackers, which are named after Captain William Clark who first saw them in 1805. And indeed, the nutcrackers can be pretty stupid. Down at Crater Lake, naturalist Donald Farner once ran a little experiment with nutcrackers. He would toss a bird several peanuts at once. The nutcracker would eat all the peanuts except one, which he prudently deposited in a nearby hole—and a jay would promptly steal it. Again and again the nutcracker would save and stash away a single peanut, which was never there when he returned to the hole. When the game ended, the nutcracker was trying to hoard a last peanut—and it was stolen too.

In the morning the nutcrackers were back for breakfast, and when we all had eaten I set out with my preteen daughters, Mary and Virginia, an older daughter Julie and her friend Rebecca Gregg to climb the basin wall behind Todd Lake. The wall was steep enough for hand-over-hand climbing and we clutched at tufts of grass and branches of slide alder as we pulled ourselves up. Hundreds of rivulets seeped out of the slope. We kept slipping in the dampness; we had trouble getting a firm foothold anywhere. When we finally scrambled to the top and sat on a fallen hemlock, we saw that the ground there was very dry—a small plateau covered with dusty pumice. Around us, the forlorn reddish leaves of ground-hugging Newberry's knotweed mingled with a few pale-blue blooms of lupine.

The plateau tilted up toward a high outcrop of rock. When we scaled it we found that the far side was an abrupt cliff. Now I could see Broken Top volcano in all its ruined grandeur, looming beyond sharp ridges, rolling alpine meadows and thinly scattered patches of trees. The shattered summit filled a large portion of the sky, a mass of pure-white snow and reddish-brown rock, blocking most of South Sister and all of Green Lakes from our view. At one time its top had been a magnificent circular crown containing the crater. But over the years a third of that crown had been breached, either eaten away slowly by weathering and glacial erosion or knocked apart by an eruption.

We stared at Broken Top a long time. In my imagination, I tried to

These young ospreys at Oregon's Crane Prairie Reservoir are about eight weeks old, and soon will leave the nest —a remarkable structure weighing about 300 pounds and strong enough to support a man. But for a few more weeks the birds' parents will keep feeding them while the youngsters are learning to catch fish for themselves.

combine it with the Three Sisters and other nearby peaks—Bachelor Butte, Husband, and Wife—into the super-volcano that the 19th Century geologist, Professor Edwin T. Hodge, believed was here one or two million years ago. He thought that lava piles had accumulated on top of a cluster of volcanoes, creating a tremendous formation he called Mount Multnomah, and that the various mountains here today are really Multnomah's eroded, emaciated remains. No other geologist has gone along with him, but then geologists are forever revising their theories as they learn more about an area. In time, Professor Hodge and his Mount Multnomah theory may prevail.

After a while the girls and I stood up, turned our backs on Broken Top and began picking our way carefully down the basin wall to our camp. Ahead and far below, Todd Lake looked like the pool in an immense Japanese garden, set off by the perfection of natural landscaping.

Hundreds of miles to the north, in the Wenatchee and Snoqualmie National Forests of Washington, the Alpine Lakes—which I have regarded since childhood as my very own—lie amid a maze of sharp peaks laced with trails. I recall dozens of them from boyhood hiking and fishing trips. But my favorite is the one called Hyas, although I have been there just twice in my life. The first time was at age eight, when my father offered me a dollar *not* to go along with him and some friends on a fishing trip. I turned down the dollar—which meant that the grownups had to take turns carrying me piggyback through deep streams that sluiced across the trail to the lake. I remember that we met nobody along the way and heard nothing but the plaintive cries of a few loons. And I remember, too, being disoriented in the morning, because the mountain peaks stood to the west, their snowfields raspberry-pink in the sun, instead of looming in dark profile against the sunrise to the east, where I was used to seeing them from Seattle. A dark forest surrounded the lake, and while my father fished, I wandered along the shore. I never went swimming—it was much too cold.

Last summer I took my wife along for my second visit to Hyas Lake. We headed east across Snoqualmie Pass, went through Roslyn, a former coal-mining town, skirted eight-mile-long Cle Elum Lake and drove up the Cle Elum River on a dirt road. We stopped twice to let young mule deer, limpid-eyed and leisurely as cows, cross in front of us. We forded two streams that flowed a foot deep over the road. (I had been carried over these same streams when the road was only a trail.) We passed a reedy flat called Fish Lake and saw something I had quite forgotten, a meadow crowded with a wild assortment of wild flowers.

Among them were tall yellow spikes of falsehellebore, drooping clusters of bleeding heart, white and yellow daisies, umbrella-shaped cow parsnips, white blooms of bunchberry dogwood, blue pennants of lupine, lavender fireweed, and scarlet flamelets of paintbrush—dozens of species, all blooming at once.

The road ended a few miles short of the lake, at a turnaround with a dozen parked cars. It developed that they all belonged to people who were hiking the Crest trail, which swings in close to the turnaround; the path to the lake itself was as deserted as it had been when I was a child. It wound past giant trees and rotting logs. On the forest floor, tree seedlings, yellow violets and ferns competed for the dim light.

At Hyas Lake the same old firs, hemlocks and pines I had known as a boy were growing right down to the shore, mingling with small alders and berry bushes. The water was dark, and I remembered that its cast had been blackish-blue before. Rainbow trout were feeding on an afternoon hatch of flies. When we gingerly edged out into the lake by walking atop a fallen log, two rainbow trout swam by to regard us, curiosities in their domain.

The lake and its shore were perfectly silent. Except for the charcoal-and-rock remains of two old campfires, there were no signs of human presence anywhere. The lake seemed bigger than I remembered and it seemed to be brooding. More likely it was I who was brooding—and reminiscing. When I looked up, beyond the solid ranks of trees on the opposite shore, I saw Cathedral Rock rearing up out of its snowfields, a monumental skyscraper of a mountain that the geological eye-blink of 50 years had not changed.

We stayed a few hours and then walked softly away from Hyas Lake to leave it in peace. We spent the night back beside the wild flowers in the meadow down the trail. I went to sleep thinking what a joy it was to find Hyas Lake—like Eagle Falls, miles away on the far side of the Alpine Lakes—still uncorrupted after I had lived most of my life between visits to it. I hoped the lake's luck, and mine, would hold until I could get back to that part of the Cascades again.

An Enchanted Alpine Lake

PHOTOGRAPHS BY HARALD SUND

When the glaciers of the last ice age retreated, about 10,000 years ago, they spangled the Cascades with a necklace of brilliant tarns, ranging in size from bathtub-sized pools up to valley-filling lakes. The most beautiful of the lakes are in the wild fastnesses near the geographical center of the state of Washington.

Here, in the upper reaches of the Stuart Range at the eastern end of this region, lies the Enchantment Lakes Basin. Within it, more than a dozen lakes—pinpoints on most maps—nestle in the crooks of elbowing ridges. Too remote to have official names, these tiny tarns are known only to a handful of wilderness votaries who have devised their own private nomenclature.

Many of the lakes and other landmarks are of such ethereal beauty that their informal names have been borrowed from mythological tales —Troll Sink, Valhalla Cirque, Lake Leprechaun, Grail Tarn and Lake Viviane, perhaps the loveliest of all. Viviane is named for the Lady of the Lake in the King Arthur legend. In one version of the story, young Arthur received his invincible sword, Excalibur, from the hand that Lady Viviane thrust forth from a fabled lake; before the King died, he or-

dered that his magic sword be taken back to her there.

The Cascades' Lake Viviane is 11 miles from the nearest road and reachable only by a taxing hike up boulder-strewn mountainsides thick with brush. Then suddenly there it is, less than 1,500 feet long, pristinely set in so perfect a microcosmic wilderness that it captures both the eye and the spirit. Its stony bottom is clearly visible some 45 feet below a surface that mirrors shimmering snowfields, icy overhangs (right), miniature alpine meadows and a formidable granitic headwall.

Snow falls here even in summer. Some remains on the ground all year round (pages 124-125), but most of it melts and encourages lush plant growth in the sheltered areas. Lyall's larch—a rare species of deciduous conifer—and whitebark pine, along with some alpine fir and mountain hemlock, grow on slopes carpeted with a colorful mixture of mosses, flowers and shrubs, such as huckleberry, juniper, heather, lupine, veronica and gentian. The greenery sprouts amid brooding glacial boulders, some as big as houses, and even manages a slim toehold on Excalibur, the sword-shaped rock that juts from the lake's northwest shore.

Lake Viviane glistens in crisp autumn sunshine, its southeastern shore curving gently at the foot of McClellan Ridge. In the foreground, water from the icy skirt of a snowfield drips onto a cylindrical rock left behind by the glacier that carved the lake's basin.

The ragged summit of Prusik Peak (left, rear), northern barrier to the Enchantment Lakes Basin, rises 1,000 feet above Lake Viviane. Squeezing through an outlet in the natural dam at center, the lake's waters plunge into Snow Creek to feed the twin Snow Lakes, partly hidden at far right.

Cascading in a shroud of spray, Lake Viviane's inlet stream splashes among lichen-spotted rocks that have been rounded by ancient glaciers, then cleft by frost action and by the rocky debris churned up in the flowing water.

A ledge of lingering summer snow arches over the lakeshore. At Viviane's altitude of nearly 7,000 feet, the snowpack lasts through the summer in the shaded areas, accumulating in some years to depths of 30 feet.

White blocks of granite, tumbled along
the lakeshore like the ruins of an
ancient castle, gleam in the noonday
sun. Among the boulders, the alpine
soil supports a ground cover of mosses
and low-growing huckleberry, and
a scattering of green whitebark pines
and autumn-gold Lyall's larches.

Early morning sun gilds the lake's 600-foot-high headwall, which reflects warm light to silhouette the eerie shapes of larch and pine.

/129

Its surface ground smooth by glaciers, a ledge of granitic rock slopes gently to the shore.

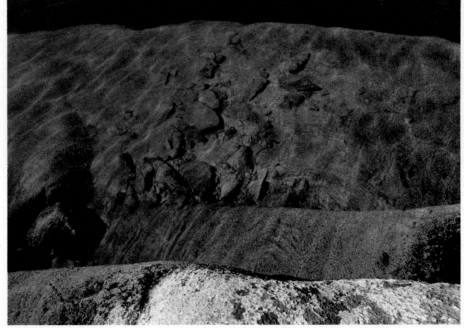

A sunken rock shelf and the lake's gravel-strewn bottom show clearly through the water.

Excalibur Rock, named for King Arthur's legendary blade, points southeastward into Lake Viviane and the Stuart Range beyond the opposite

shore. Cracks in the rock provide rootholds for plants like the Lyall's larch seedling (foreground) that is turning yellow from fall's first frosts.

5/ Underworld of the Cascades

The lava beds stretch...incongruously through the
green country, best seen in the early evening when the light
plays fanciful tricks with the forms and tones of
this ancient cataclysm.   NANCY WILSON ROSS/ FARTHEST REACH

On the southeast flank of the Cascades the landscape contains some
strange and often disconcerting phenomena. In times not long past, volcanic upheavals created bizarre effects upon the earth's surface, and
today the region's ground water and the vestigial volcanism produce
unique and startling effects both above the surface and beneath it.
Among these are lakes that feel warm as tub water to the touch; traces
of long-vanished forests whose trees have left detailed imprints like
those on plaster molds within the frozen rock; and rivers that spring in
full flow straight from fissures in the ground. In addition the southeast
Cascades are strewn with lava beds as bleak as moonscapes and with
cinder cones that rise hundreds of feet above the ground, while here
and there the earth has been gored by streams of lava that left behind tubular caves as capacious as railroad tunnels.

The heart of this peculiarly fascinating part of the Cascades is the
land around Mount Newberry in the Deschutes National Forest. Mount
Newberry once was a broad-shouldered volcano, standing some 9,000
feet high; its total mass—about 80 cubic miles—was as great as that of
California's Mounts Shasta and Shastina put together. Newberry had
built itself up as a shield volcano of the gently sloping Mauna Loa type,
having gradually increased its height and mass through the repeated up-
welling of many thin layers of lava that oozed from deep within the
earth. Then, about 20,000 years ago, during a series of violent erup-

tions, Mount Newberry collapsed inward of its own weight, leaving a huge crater that now holds East Lake and Paulina Lake. In the course of that cataclysmic collapse, the mountain disrupted and stopped up the miles of conduits that had carried lava up from its depths. Later eruptions, some occurring within the past 1,000 to 2,000 years, have burst to the surface at more than 150 points nearby to form parasitic cinder cones rising 200 to 500 feet above the ground. The raw material for these cones emanated from the same subterranean chambers as the material for Mount Newberry itself, popping through the surface at points of least resistance.

Another and, to me, even more fascinating memento of Newberry's hell-fire youth is Lavacicle Cave, into which forest ranger Terry Virgin and I wormed our way one July morning. We barely fit through the entrance, which was just a crack in the desert floor. We twisted inside head first, wriggling on our stomachs over a long bed of fine pumice sand, pushing our gas lanterns ahead of us, keeping our hard hats and our backsides low to avoid scraping them against the rock ceiling less than a foot over our heads.

After 100 feet or so, the sand floor descended or the ceiling lifted —we couldn't tell which—and we were able to crawl on all fours and then to stand erect. Where we stood, the cavern was shaped like a cross-section of a skull, with the cranial dome symmetrically rounded on both sides and across the top. The rock walls were smooth, but marked by horizontal striations. Three-inch shelves stood out about five feet up both walls, marking where molten lava had poured through here more than 1,000 years ago.

Lavacicle Cave actually is a lava tube, formed when a river of incandescent rock cooled first on its outside surfaces—which hardened into a crust—and then drained from the inside like a garden hose. In some places massive rockfalls have all but blocked the inside of the tube, leaving only narrow crawl spaces over or around piles of boulders. None of these cave-ins, however, has created any new entrances, although at spots the ceiling is only a few feet underground.

The Cascades hold many of these intriguing caves; some, like Ape Cave south of Mount Saint Helens, are several miles long. At one time the conduit that is now Lavacicle Cave lay on the surface of the earth. But over the centuries it gradually was covered by drifting soil, ash and pumice, until the volcanic tube was entirely underground. Lavacicle was not discovered until 1959 when two men in a Forest Service crew, cleaning up after a forest fire, stumbled across the entrance.

From the place where we could first stand, the cave extended half a mile under the earth, curving gently downhill to a point where the floor, an accumulation of centuries of water-borne grit from surface fractures and wind-blown sand from the entrance, met the roof. Halfway to this dead end we came upon the curious formations from which Lavacicle gets its name: lava stalactites hanging like icicles from the ceiling. In addition, there were stalagmites rising from the floor, looking like colonies of miniature skyscrapers and toy castles. All had been created by fluid lava that kept dripping after some superheated torrent of rock, propelled by gases from a volcano or earth fissure, swept past. The final drips, looking as fresh and glistening as syrup, still hang where they hardened above, or perch atop the little structures below.

The formations are beautiful and are as hard as any conventional rock. They also represent a good reason not to wander this lava tube without a companion or extra sources of light. If you were alone in here, and your flashlight or gas lantern burned out, one stumble in the dark could easily result in a broken leg, and that could be the end of you. Few people ever visit Lavacicle and fewer still venture this far into it. Terry Virgin suggested that we extinguish our lanterns for a minute to find out just how dark and silent the cave is. We did. It was as utterly black and still as a tomb. I turned, and accidentally kicked a tiny rock castle. A two-inch crenelated tower broke off with a tinkle that echoed up and down the cavernous corridor. We relighted our lanterns, and a short while later crawled back outside.

Later that day Terry and I explored a different sort of lava tube, the South Ice Cave, about 15 miles southwest of Lavacicle. This chilly underground passage is known as an ice cave not because it is carved out of solid ice, like those on Mount Rainier, but because it is cold enough in winter to freeze the water that seeps in through its shell of volcanic rock. Winter temperatures in the south Cascades are frequently below zero; even in summer the temperature in the cave rarely rises much above freezing, and ice that forms in winter never entirely melts.

The entrance to South Ice Cave is through a 50-foot-wide natural foyer created when the cave roof collapsed, opening up the side of the mountain. As Terry and I walked in, two brownish-gray bats glided out. We had, apparently, ruined the sleep and upset the schedules of a couple of lump-nosed bats, the most nocturnal of all Cascade animals. The bat's unlovely nickname was inspired by glandular growths on its face that give it something of the appearance of the late J. P. Morgan. It is also more flatteringly known as Townsend's big-eared bat, or the jack-rabbit bat, because of its inch-long ears—which are about a quarter the length of its whole body. A convivial sleeper, it usually spends the day huddled with others of its kind in a clump the size of a bushel basket and seldom ventures from its preferred habitat, an abandoned mine shaft or a cave like this one, until well after dark.

Just inside the entrance we interrupted a tanager and half a dozen sparrows at their bath in a puddle, and they fluttered, cheeping, out into the nearby pine trees. A cold draft of air blew into our faces from deep within the cave.

Farther inside we saw that the South Ice Cave was not as uniformly tubular as Lavacicle. The interior was majestically galleried, with tunnels as wide as driveways leading to higher and lower levels where many lava streams had flowed together. Our path was crooked, a long series of up-and-down climbs over an obstacle course of massive and slippery lava blocks that seismic tremors or frost action—or both—had dislodged from the ceiling.

The rocks felt cold and slippery, and when we shone our lanterns on them we saw that they were glazed with ice. We sloshed through inch-deep meltwater that covered the floor. I dipped a finger into the water; it had a strong taste of iron and an aftertaste of sulfur (from mineral solutions it picked up flowing over the lava). Farther inside we skidded over larger pools, frozen as solid and glassy-slick as skating rinks. Guiding each other with our beams of light, Terry and I used lava outcroppings and four-foot-long icicles for handholds as we gingerly slithered across these small lakes. Once I slipped and fell, almost losing my lantern, and shot across the tube until I jolted into a stalactite of ice at the edge of a rockfall that sloped down steeply a dozen feet. Finally, we were stopped by yet another rockfall that seemed to block off the rest of the cave. Terry said there was a barely passable way around the barrier, but on the far side there was just more rock and ice.

An eerie, shivery place it was, seemingly fit only for bats and such eldritch creatures as the ice cricket, which lives both in and outside caves. This rare and primitive insect—most of whose close relatives have been extinct for millions of years—still hangs on in a few areas like eastern Siberia, the mountains of Japan and some parts of Western North America, including the Cascades. Pale, wingless and only about as long as a paper clip, the ice cricket creeps about preying on other insects. It is happiest at about 38°F., a temperature at which most insects become dormant. Under these circumstances, the ice cricket must have an easy

Lavacicle Cave (left) in central Oregon was once a river of fluid rock. As its outer layer cooled and hardened, the still-molten interior rock drained away, leaving a tunnel studded with lava stalactites and stalagmites. These intricately fluted lavacicles, some of them three feet tall and up to six inches thick, were formed by the slow dripping and cooling of residual lava.

time overcoming any live banquet it encounters. But the low temperature also somewhat limits the food supply—a fact that may help to account for the ice cricket's rarity.

Among other creatures that have been found in lava caves are a few pale, blind and truly troglodytic specimens. Some of the more unusual include the matchstick-sized millipede; a fly that sips water from puddles on cave floors; and a variety of daddy longlegs—which somehow managed over the centuries to adapt to cave life, even though its usual diet consists of dead insects and plant juices.

Long before white men came to the Cascades, the Indians found caves like this one to be perfect refrigerators for game they killed. Later on, white settlers were grateful for these year-round sources of ice. In the early 1900s, horse-drawn wagons from Bend, Oregon, creaked 12 miles over dusty tracks to Arnold Ice Cave, picked up blocks of ice, and carried them back to town to help the inhabitants endure the scorching days of summer.

Emerging from the darkness of South Ice Cave was like stepping from a cold-storage locker into an oven. The temperature outside was in the high 80s and the afternoon sunlight was blindingly bright. There had been rain a few days before and all the plants of the ponderosa-forest floor, washed clean of dust, had responded almost overnight. Long beds of dwarf purple monkeyflower and woolly sunflower were in bloom beside the trail. Clumps of bitterbrush, rabbit brush, squaw currant and desert ocean spray, growing in the soft shade of the pines, had turned from gray to green. Even the dust-colored sagebrush, called *Artemisia tridentata* after its three-tipped leaves, had soaked up moisture and put on a pale green cast. Such signs of life, and the sun itself, were terribly welcome after our long immersion in the black deadness of a place where only creatures of the dark are at home.

Lava Cast Forest, 20 miles north of South Ice Cave, is another strange byproduct of volcanism. The place is so desolate, even on a bright, cheerful summer day, that the impression is of some other, lifeless planet. Lava Cast is, in reality, a ghost forest, populated by the death masks of trees. Six thousand years ago, a large stand of ponderosa pine flourished here. Then a fissure opened in the side of Mount Newberry and a flood of lava poured out. By the time the lava reached the pine grove, the rock tide was 20 feet deep, a viscous, slow-moving mass. It flowed over fallen trees, knocked down many living trees and covered them too, and left a few of the larger pines standing—briefly. Though cooling rapidly, the lava was still hot enough to roast any tree or bush that it touched and turn it to charcoal.

Even after white men began to frequent the region, nobody paid any special attention to the strange humps and holes in this particular lava field. The few men who bothered to think about the odd formations took them for blowouts—irregularities created by gases in the lava —and let it go at that. Finally the late Walter J. Perry, poet and naturalist, thought to examine the insides of some of these oddly symmetrical shafts and found imprinted there the distinctive, reptile-skin pattern of ponderosa bark, and he appropriately named the area the Lava Cast Forest.

On a green knoll beyond the lava casts, I saw ancient living pines, probably descendants of survivors of that holocaust. The dead forest was struggling to come back to life. A few small trees had taken root in chinks in the lava, and some brave splashes of Indian paintbrush were blooming there. As time went by and more soil formed on the exposed lava surfaces, other plant invaders would take hold. Perhaps one day another stand of ponderosa would conceal the devastation.

Having seen the lava's effects from underground and on the surface, I decided to seek an overview and thus, the next morning, after several hours' climb, I stood at the summit of nearby Paulina Peak. Higher than Newberry Crater, the 7,984-foot summit is a lonely spot with a magnificent view up and down the southern Cascades. On this July day the nearest snow in sight was on the 9,000-foot dome of Bachelor Butte, 30 miles to the northwest. Where I stood, the ubiquitous paintbrush and some purple rock penstemon were flowering and a turkey vulture idled in the warm air overhead.

From my vantage at the crest, overlooking the jumbled manifestations of past upheaval, I caught sight of yet one more startling vestige of the volcanic past. This was North America's largest outpouring of obsidian, a jet-black volcanic glass so hard that it can be used in jewelry. Obsidian is a relatively rare kind of volcanic byproduct that begins as a rhyolitic lava rich in silicates and that can contain up to 10 per cent water. This admixture of water helps to keep the lava fluid even under great pressure in the earth's depths—and at relatively low temperatures, too. When a volcano squirts out some of this kind of lava into the atmosphere, the water vaporizes and the lava, already fairly cool, solidifies too quickly to allow large crystals to form. The result, unlike the coarse, bubbly common lava rock, is gleaming black glass with smooth curved surfaces and sharp edges. I was looking now at a mile-

More than six feet of ice—the accumulation of centuries of seepage—coats the floor of Oregon's South Ice Cave.

long obsidian mass that had slithered out of a vent or fissure long after Mount Newberry's collapse to form a gleaming, fascinating curve between East Lake and Paulina Lake.

I made my way to the black cliff where the obsidian river had stopped a few feet from a pine woods, and I climbed to the top. Thousands of shards of the black glassy rock brilliantly reflected the sun, and under my boots tiny pieces tinkled like broken china. The flow is still mostly empty of vegetation; only a few patches of green-and-gold lichen coat the dark surfaces. Obsidian weathers slowly. After cooling, its surface absorbs minute amounts of water (the age of a flow can be determined by the amount of absorption) but not enough to give frost action the leverage it needs to break up other kinds of rocks. For many centuries to come, there will be little soil here.

In the past, Indians used obsidian as knives and scrapers. Properly chipped and shaped, obsidian shards made splendidly efficient—and dangerous—arrowheads.

That afternoon, down in Newberry's crater, I walked a mile along the shore of East Lake. There I noted a faintly sulfurous, rotten-egg smell, and at several points a few feet out from the dark-sand beach, gas bubbles were rising among floating aquatic plants. The water was warm to the touch. When I thrust my hand into the bottom sand, my fingers became warmer the farther down they groped. Terry told me that a few feet below where I could reach, he has recorded temperatures of 154°F. This means that Newberry is not quite dead—any more than are Lassen and Rainier. Here was a potent reminder that the earth's inner fires still rage beneath the crust. Their heat rises near the surface at points like this in the Cascades, hinting at the uncontrollable forces that can create or wipe out entire mountains.

Throughout this end of the Cascades, water, like lava, moves underground in mysterious—and forceful—ways. The Metolius and Fall rivers, for example, rise 40 miles from each other, at about 5,000 feet elevation, on the eastern slope of the mountains. And they rush from the hillsides suddenly, full-blown, and then glide away gracefully through glades of ponderosas.

Both rivers are clean, fresh and clear—and their sources are unknown. One theory is that their water comes from a glacier on the west side of the Cascades, and that the rivers somehow have tunneled under the mountains to reappear here on the dry east side. A more probable explanation is that they are fed by snowmelt that percolates down from nearby buttes and is filtered pure by passing through masses of volcanic rock. In any case, the rivers' volume is unusually constant, the same in fall as in spring, in the morning as in the afternoon.

The Metolius is a great fly-fishing stream (once full of native Chinook salmon, rainbow trout and whitefish), now stocked only with rainbows from the Wizard Falls hatchery. One day, I set out from secluded Camp Sherman, four miles south of the hatchery, to walk upstream to a mystic place known as Head of the Metolius. All along the river, the trail was dappled with the shade of great yellow pines. The Metolius here flows briskly, past little islands crowded with wild flowers; it is as dignified and businesslike as an English countryside stream. I reached the river's head after an easy hike, and stared into the bushy hillside where the water gushes forth from great fissures, as though spewing from a ruptured main. I knelt, dipped a hand in the water and drank; it was cold and almost sweetly pure to the taste.

Fall River is smaller, springing unexpectedly out of the woods near a forest ranger station to the south of the Metolius. Like the Metolius, Fall River is a good trout stream, coursing past flower-decked islets to flow off through the forest, keeping its secret to itself. Both rivers feed into the Deschutes—which is also a considerable geographic curiosity. The many and various forks at its headwaters flow from every major compass direction. Then the main Deschutes begins to behave like a normal river, heading north toward the Columbia, which it enters three miles below the old Indian fish-spearing spot of Celilo Falls.

Another unique south Cascade river, the Rogue, reaches the Pacific via a major detour all its own. The Rogue's headwaters are on the northern edge of Crater Lake National Park, where a prehistoric lava flow blocked the river in its tracks 6,600 years ago. However, the Rogue eventually ate its way through the volcanic rock. I walked on solid lava across its burrow a few feet from where the river dives underground. I could hear the Rogue underfoot, hammering its way down a tunnel of its own making. The river reappears several hundred yards downstream, boils angrily into full sight and continues its roughshod course to the sea—offering along the way some of the nation's best steelhead fishing. In time, it will wash away the lava, grain by rock grain, and resume the aboveground course that the eruption so rudely interrupted.

One more monument to volcanism remained for me to explore—the red-tinted natural fortress called Fort Rock. Rising from the earth like a great crusted crown in the High Lava Plains on the east side of the Or-

This obsidian cataract on Mount Newberry was formed some 1,350 years ago, when silica-rich lava, spilling down the side of the mountain, cooled quickly. Now, amid great chunks of the glittering black natural glass, a 20-foot-high pine tree struggles—as it has for two centuries—to survive.

egon Cascades, Fort Rock is about 300 feet high and half a mile wide, and can be seen for miles. Many legends have developed about it. Some relate that peaceful Indians hid here from attackers; others that emigrant wagon trains hid here from less peaceful Indians. In fact, the somewhat tattered crown is so huge that at least a battalion of armed men would be required to defend it.

Technically, Fort Rock is a tuff ring, the remains of an old volcano, made up of compressed volcanic fragments. Tens of thousands of years ago, after the volcano had died and disappeared, a large lake covered the desert here. Waves whipped up by storms on the lake cut vertical cliffs on one side of the rock circle and eroded away the other. Today, cows and horses wandering the range frequently take shelter from harsh winter weather beneath some of the overhangs that were carved by the prehistoric lake.

Fort Rock has become one of the most important archeological sites in the United States. About 40 years ago, L. S. Cressman, an Oregon anthropologist, found some ancient sandals in one of the recesses in the natural wall. Students joined him at the dig; after a while they unearthed 75 sandals—and ever since then the site has been known as the shoe store. Some of the sandals were still caked with mud from the lake, others had been scorched by walking on hot pumice.

The sandals were woven with cord made from strands of sagebrush bark. Because of this use of bark fibers, scientists could determine the age of the shoes by carbon-14 dating. Tests proved that the Fort Rock people lived more than 9,000 years ago. Subsequent digging at the sandal site and in nearby caves uncovered charcoal bits among arrowheads, rude tools and weights for fishing nets; this evidence pushed the date of human habitation here back to at least 13,200 years ago.

From all the archeological evidence, it appears that the Fort Rock people had a hard life. They did some hunting for game with crude darts and spears, but they existed primarily as foragers on roots, nuts, seeds, berries and wild fruit. Apparently they never thought of using the skins of slain animals for clothes; their only garments were made of grass and bark, remnants of which were found in the sites. Their existence was a constant struggle against starvation and the elements, and lives were correspondingly short—probably not extending more than 18 or 20 years, shorter by a decade or more than their primitive counterparts in post-ice-age Europe.

Like stone-age peoples elsewhere, however, the Fort Rock hunters were artists. Archeologists have found a painting in red pigment of a spear thrower in a cave. Interestingly, the top of the spear is notched with several rows of white, perhaps indicating the artist's prowess as a hunter. And Fort Rock society seems to have been formally divided along sexual lines. During his excavations, Cressman found one sheltered cave, overlooking the now-extinct lake, where hunters, presumably male, had sat together around a fire and chipped away at their obsidian knives. "This is a place where men hung out," Cressman has said. "There is no evidence of housekeeping tools. They are in another cave, 100 yards away."

Despite so much evidence, the ultimate fate of the Fort Rock hunters remains a mystery. Some archeologists believe they may have been killed or chased away about 3,000 to 4,000 years ago by other, more sophisticated hunters who had primitive bows and arrows. But no one is sure what happened to the early men living at Fort Rock.

In the course of investigating the archeological sites and the geology of Fort Rock, my teen-age son Robert and I one afternoon clambered out onto an overlook atop one of the cliffs. Below us, sagebrush flatland sloped up toward Paulina Peak to the north. In the distance two hawks circled, hunting as a team, and off to the east a rancher's truck barreled across the desert, leaving a long rooster tail of dust. Somewhere beyond the dust was a man I wanted to see—Reuben Long. I had heard he owned Fort Rock itself until he gave it to the state of Oregon as a park and to the federal government as a national monument.

Reub has spent most of his 76 years in the lava-littered landscape on this side of the Cascades. He was raised in a homesteader's cabin here and started working as a cowhand when he was 12. He took time out to run a pool hall in the nearby town of Silver Lake when he was 16, and has since made his living as a bronco rider, packer for dudes, horse trader and rancher.

We caught up with Reub in the late afternoon. His beat-up camper was outside a corral at an abandoned homestead on a crooked wagon trail. A strapping, leathery hulk of a man, Reub filled the back doorway when he welcomed us. He happened to be out here with a friend to mend some fences and to look after a few horses he pastures nearby. He was just cleaning up after supper.

I told Reub and the friend that we had stopped at Fort Rock on the way over and the friend said, "Giving that to the country is the least of what Reub has done. Why, he's given away more land around here than most ranchers ever own." The friend was a wizened, retired steel-

Early morning frost dusts the crests of lava waves, whose troughs are as much as 12 feet deep. Part of a 10-square-mile lava flow that pushed the Deschutes River from its original channel, this vast bed of rock is so desolate that astronauts visited it to experience a moonlike environment.

worker turned cowhand named Jay Scheidecker, and he sidled past us to take a bucket over to a windmill, the only operating piece of equipment on the homestead. He walked stiffly, with a double limp, the way some cowboys do.

As the evening grew dark, Reub told us to make ourselves at home and spread our sleeping bags on the ground. A coyote barked as we went to sleep. Just before dawn a chorus of coyotes awakened us; they were singing to each other, all the notes well above middle C. The long, drawn-out cries seemed to come from all directions. There was no telling how close the coyotes were. When there is no wind, the crisp desert air can play tricks with your ear, making a sound from far away seem to come from right over your shoulder.

In the morning Reub called us to breakfast: strong coffee, of course, and scrambled eggs mixed with chopped-up leftover hot dogs, fried in an unidentifiable kind of shortening. In a case like this I always ask for black pepper and use plenty of it.

After breakfast Reub invited us to go with him to see a place called Devil's Garden. He jounced the camper over the faintest of tracks, through brush and across bare black pavements of lava. We kept flushing jack rabbits, which went bounding away through the grass, and we overtook one coyote. Trotting along on our right, it crossed casually in front of us, glancing at the camper with its left eye. Smaller than a wolf and having large pointed ears and a spry, graceful gait, the coyote resembled a bleached, slightly hangdog version of a German shepherd. (Besides looking like a dog, the coyote leaves tracks so similar to a dog's that even expert trappers can barely tell them apart.) After a moment it slipped through the roadside fence, and two seconds later it was invisible in the sagebrush.

Around here coyotes are rarely shot. They are too useful, keeping down the populations of gophers, jack rabbits, field mice and other rodents. With plenty of volcanic rocks around to den-up in, plenty of food for the litters of pups that are whelped in springtime, and plenty of human tolerance for their right to exist, the wild dogs have become almost tame, still wary but not always on the run. Besides eating fresh meat, the coyote, *Canis latrans*, devours carrion, although at times in the fall it has to make do with grasshoppers. In the depths of the winter, when its feet frequently bleed agonizingly from ice cuts, it has trouble finding anything to eat at all.

After a few miles we got to the Devil's Garden, a sprawling collection of small spatter cones, domes, lava tubes and blowouts—all coexisting in an inchoate collection of rocks with sage, grass, brittlebrush, an unusual small-leafed shrub called desert sweet, and wild flowers that seemed hand-planted in the piles of lava. The garden was formed more than 7,000 years ago when lava poured out of two vents in a fairly quiet fashion—not at all like the fiery fountains that spewed from some major Cascade volcanoes—and then cooled into a ropy texture on the ground. The whole area, now dusty and well weathered, looks markedly inhospitable: like some of the other lava fields in this part of the Cascades it appears to be more of a forlorn moonscape than a fit place for man or beast.

Off to one side, Reub showed us an eight-foot circle of lava rocks. "There are a number of these around here," he said. "I figure the Indians used them to hold down their tepees and keep the wind out." We did not question the authenticity of the circles as artifacts. But knowing Reub a little, I kept wondering whether, at some time during his three score years, he might have arranged these "tepee rings" as one of his little jokes. I would never suggest this to his face; as lord of the rings and of all the rest of this domain, he might take offense.

In any event, the true story of the tepee rings remains for me a fascinating mystery, as does the fate of the Fort Rock hunters, and the source of the Fall and Metolius rivers. I will remain intrigued, too, by the black, silent lava tubes and other underground land forms in this part of the Cascades. They all have their secrets; they are entirely distinct from the rest of this vast, expansive mountain range—and from most other spots on earth.

6/ The Wild, Wild North

Every ridge opens visions that halt one in his steps and produce sheer wonder and amazement.... There are peaks too numerous to count. Each one is a study in elegance and distinction. WILLIAM O. DOUGLAS/ MY WILDERNESS

From the ground or from the air, the North Cascades look like what they are—the wildest part of this whole mountain range. From Snoqualmie Pass on up to the Fraser River in the extreme north, sharp peaks march rank on rank, their shoulders caped with snow for most of the year. These mountains rise precipitously, almost straight up, from flat-floored, heavily glaciated valleys. Within this primitive landscape, deeply gashed by rivers, there are more glaciers, more trees, more lakes and more wildlife than in any other portion of the range. Paradoxically this part of the Cascade wilderness is under the greatest pressure from civilization. All but uninhabited, the mountains here stand within sight —and an hour's travel—of millions of people.

One day in early September, I had a bird's-eye view of the Cascades on a 350-mile wilderness flight. Though the day before had been cloudy and rainy, I was lucky enough to have an interval of fine, clear weather for the trip. (Around Seattle we used to say you could be *fairly* sure of the sun on any one day between July Fourth and Labor Day—if you were lucky.) What was more, I had the best guide I could have hoped for: J. Stewart Lowther of the University of Puget Sound in Tacoma. By nature he is an environmentalist, a devotee of wild places; by trade a geologist and paleontologist. He had offered to share with me his expertise and his single-engined Cessna 172 for my aerial reconnaissance.

With Stewart at the controls, we took off from the tiny Bellevue airport near Seattle and headed east toward Snoqualmie Pass. Mount Rainier was off to our right, its rounded top tinted the palest pink in the morning light. The countryside below spread out in folds of wooded hills, some of them crazy-quilted by open patches, called clear-cuts, in the forest, where loggers had swept out every sizable tree. We passed 4,167-foot Mount Si, a monolithic knob of rock, and looked for traces of the mountain goats that graze its bleak slopes; but we couldn't see any. Then, at Snoqualmie Pass, we turned northeast. The summit area, mauled by highway and ski-resort construction, was an ugly mass of scar tissue on the land, but once we left it behind there was no sign whatever of civilization.

Flying into the Alpine Lakes region, I picked out a sliver of turquoise among dozens of bright blue pools. It was Hyas Lake at the base of Cathedral Rock. Here, during the past summer, my wife Mary and I had found, still unspoiled, a flowered meadow I had visited in my childhood. The summer flowers would be gone by now. Instead I could see small splashes of red as vine maples began to turn color for fall.

We skimmed a sea of white-capped peaks, where glaciers hung like breaking waves over deep valley troughs. I lost count of the glaciers, but I knew there were 767 in the North Cascades, and that each fall geologists take an aerial inventory of these slowly moving ice masses to measure their advances or retreats. Soon we were over Lake Chelan, a 55-mile-long, narrow, twisting ribbon of water. At the south end of the lake the hills are gentle and bare, crossed by roads and filled with vacation homes. At the more isolated north end, however, the mountains are high and menacing; the two small settlements there, Stehekin and Lucerne, can be reached only by boat, plane or a long hike. A few miles of Park Service and Forest Service roads extend out from both villages, but most ground travel here is over a network of trails.

Earlier in the summer, naturalist Jim Anderson and I had packed out from Lucerne with Chris Comstock, a district Forest Service ranger. We had struck westward, climbing along a staircase of lakes that leads toward the crest of the range. A few minutes along the trail a blue-gray blur startled us, streaking past soundlessly only 10 feet away and three feet above the ground.

"A goshawk," Jim said, "the largest forest hawk in the West. He's probably spotted a blue grouse; that's his prey of choice. I once had a goshawk for a hunting bird. In Germany, the old falconers called them pothawks because with a goshawk doing the hunting, they were always sure of getting something for the dinner pot."

The trail led us along the base of a cliff, in and out of dry brush and trees. We passed five-foot-tall stalks of Sitka columbine, gone to seed, and fading lavender blooms of fireweed. We also walked by a few dark pockets in the cliffs across the creek where miners once dug; a miner's tilted one-room shack sat abandoned down below, overgrown by trees.

"There's an interesting plant succession in this valley," Chris Comstock remarked. "Avalanches have a lot to do with it. We just passed through an extremely old stand of Douglas fir, but right here we're in a little pocket of lodgepole pine, where a slide came down. The lodgepoles, along with the cottonwoods and the aspens, are the pioneering trees in a newly exposed area." He added that the climax tree species here, as on the Pacific side of the Cascades, is the shade-tolerant western hemlock, which sooner or later replaces all others—unless an avalanche, a fire or a logger clears an area and gives other tree seedlings some additional sunlight.

We walked past a beaver pond that was marshy and studded with dead trees. The cottonwoods and aspens around the shore looked as though they had been chopped off about eight feet above the ground. Chris explained that snow had covered the trunks to that height the winter before, and beavers had chewed through the wood above the snow to get raw material for their dams. I was surprised to learn the beavers prefer summer weather—not because they dislike the cold, but because their dark fur, when outlined against the snow, is an easily spotted target for predators. In the heavy vegetation of summer, however, beavers are well camouflaged.

Next to the pond, Jim Anderson pointed to a 3-by-10-inch hole neatly gouged out of a thick conifer. It was the trademark of the pileated woodpecker. I had seen this bird in the Olympic Mountains but never in the Cascades. Measuring 18 inches from its red crest to the tip of its tail feathers, it is the biggest of Western woodpeckers, and has the longest and sharpest beak. "When one pecks away at a tree," Jim said, "it is precision chiseling, like jackhammering; the bird is either hunting for food or making a nesting cavity large enough to squeeze into. The ground, as you see here, becomes littered with ten-inch-long splinters and other chunks of wood."

We paused a few times to pick huckleberries or to admire sprays of glossy, carmine-colored—and poisonous—western baneberries. After another hour or so of dawdling up the trail, we reached Hart Lake. The water appeared butterscotch-colored in the fading late-afternoon light.

In July and August, mountain meadows and glades bloom with all sizes, shapes and shades of alpine flowers. On the slopes of Mount Rainier, the tall Cascades azalea appears, along with vivid spikes of lupine and tiny shooting stars. Half the way up Mount Hood flourish the pale avalanche lily and the Washington lily—the latter never found, curiously, in its namesake state.

SUBALPINE LUPINE

WASHINGTON LILY

AVALANCHE LILY

JEFFREY SHOOTING STAR

CASCADES AZALEA

For a while we could see upvalley to where a waterfall poured lazily out of Lyman Lake four miles away. Above it, clouds were gathering around Glacier Peak, the wind was rising and a storm was brewing. The weather is always treacherous up here: a balmy late-summer day can quickly turn into a gale of wind and rain or snow, carried by a storm careening around some mountain. We decided to stop where we were. We hurriedly gathered firewood from a shattered tangle of big cottonwood trees that had been felled, all in the same downhill direction, by an avalanche. By the time our fire was going, the waterfall was hidden by clouds and a hard rain was falling.

I had brought along a large plastic tarpaulin and we needed all hands to tie it down to rocks and trees as the wind kept tearing it from our grasp. We heated and ate cans of beef stew, then huddled together in our yellow lean-to. When one of us ventured out to put a log on the fire, he would be wet and shivering when he came back inside the shelter. For hours, noisy sheets of rain whipped past us. The tarpaulin deflected most of the water and wind, but we got little sleep.

By morning the storm, an overture to winter, had passed. We could see in the first rays of the sun that the heights above us, where the wind had come from, were dusted with fresh snow. The storm had worn itself out moving across the mountains; later in the day, back down at Lucerne, we were told that not a drop of rain had fallen there during the night.

Not far from Lucerne one day in early July, I had my first close-up encounter with a bear. Walking alone in the Chelan Mountains, I had wandered off the trail to follow the skittering uphill flight of a flame-colored tortoise-shell butterfly. It must have broken out of the protective coloring of its chrysalis only a few hours earlier, because it was still flying uncertainly, stopping often to rest on twigs or to warm its wings on a sunstruck rock. Yet whenever my footfall or shadow drew near, the butterfly took off, luring me deeper into the brush. The insect I was chasing was not alone. After a few minutes I saw more tortoise-shells, and then came upon a patch of ceanothus bushes that had been stripped almost leafless. Inch-long, bluish-gray chrysalises were dangling from the few remaining leaves and bare twigs. Each was suspended by a tube, like the stem of a tiny plum. Some were nearly transparent, displaying the orange-and-black coloring of butterflies-to-be inside their cases. A few were swaying as young tortoise-shells struggled to break free from the prisons that had formed around them weeks before, when they were

A black-bear cub about four months old, not long out of the den, scrambles for safety up a pine tree. A cub this age weighs about 20 pounds and is a much faster climber than his ungainly 300-pound mother; she will chase him up a tree when danger approaches.

still caterpillars. While they remained in the caterpillar stage, the tortoise-shells had been storing up energy by defoliating the shrubs; as butterflies, they would suck their sustenance from flowers, pollinating them in the process.

I brushed against a branch and two triangular, black, leaflike shapes fluttered to the ground. They were newly emerged butterflies, their wings folded back tightly so the dark bottom surfaces could serve as protective coloration among the surrounding leaves. A step ahead of me, in a shaft of morning sunlight, I saw that this defense mechanism had failed one insect. A yellow jacket had killed a tortoise-shell before it could take flight, and was gnawing on its body. Earlier, I had seen wasps harass some white butterflies in a thicket of snowy-blossomed wild blackberries among the western foothills of the Cascades. No sooner would a butterfly land on a flower than a wasp or two would zing down and frighten it into a flight for its life.

I headed back downhill, crashing through some undergrowth and jumping the last yard onto the trail. There, a full-grown black bear stood stock-still 30 feet away, looking at me. Evidently I had interrupted its berrypicking, but I certainly did not want to annoy it any further. Standing on all fours, it was at least three feet tall at the shoulder, massive, glossy-coated and calm of eye. It could easily have outrun or outclimbed me, so there was no point in flight. We faced each other for a few seconds—and then it simply trotted away without a backward glance; the bear probably was far less disconcerted by our unexpected confrontation than I was.

I had run into other bears in the Cascades, but none so big or so near to me. Up at Ross Lake, not far from the Canadian border, I once heard a deep-throated bellowing; I looked across the water and saw a black bear clawing with great delight at a stump that must have been full of beetles and bugs. Concentrating on its meal, it did not pay the slightest attention to me. Most black bears tend to treat people this way, either ignoring them, or ambling quietly in the opposite direction. Another Cascade native, however, the grizzly bear, tends to behave in quite a different fashion. Though I have never actually seen one, for the sad and simple reason that the species has been hunted and harassed to the point of extinction, the grizzly still appears on the checklist of animals in the North Cascades National Park. Yet in these wild forests I always sense the possibility of encountering a grizzly. If I do, I hope it is at a distance. For grizzlies, which weigh half a ton and stand nine feet tall, often attack without warning—and the attack is deadly.

Almost all of the early wilderness men who came this way held the grizzly in awe and some fear. Members of the Lewis and Clark expedition, which traversed the Cascades along the Columbia, were several times chased by grizzlies. Meriwether Lewis described them as a "furious and formidable animal," which "will frequently pursue the hunter when wounded." Lewis later wrote in his diary, "I must confess that I do not like the grizzly and had rather fight two Indians than one bear." Lewis and Clark's men once shot a grizzly no less than 10 times (five times in the chest), and it still survived for 20 minutes before bleeding to death. That particular bear weighed 600 pounds, was almost nine feet tall, four feet around the neck, and its claws measured more than four inches long.

Just 100 years ago, thousands of grizzlies prowled the Pacific Northwest, but hunters rapidly exterminated them. In Oregon alone, one party of five professional hunters killed 700 grizzlies during 1848. By the turn of the century, only five or six grizzlies remained in the entire state of Washington. Though occasional sightings are still reported, the last-known grizzly killed in the Cascades was shot by one Evan Stoneman on September 14, 1931, on the banks of Chesnimnus Creek in northern Oregon.

Like the grizzly, the timber wolf (*Canis lupus*) appears on the park's official checklist—but not, alas, on my own life list. If there truly are any survivors in the Cascades, they probably spend most of their time across the international boundary in British Columbia, where human interlopers are even rarer than they are in the North Cascades. Wolves both like and need the protection of deep wilderness. They are creatures of habit, to the point that a hunter can set his watch by a wolf's schedule. If a wolf passes a certain rock at 2 o'clock one afternoon, it will be there at 2 o'clock the next day—a characteristic that has made the wolf easy to decimate.

Why man has always felt this impulse to kill wolves remains a mystery to me. Maybe it is simply because wolves *look* scary, and sound scary, with their unearthly call. Whatever the reason, all over the world wolves have always been killed on sight, to the accompaniment of fright stories—e.g., the Big Bad Wolf—to justify the slaughter.

A wolf indeed will kill readily enough for food, but there is no authenticated case of a wolf attacking a human unless the person was between the wolf and its young and was, therefore, considered a threat to the family. In any human society this protective impulse toward the family would be considered a virtue. And, indeed, the wolf is a devoted family animal, seldom roaming alone or far from its relatives. Male or female, it is a willing and indulgent parent; a pack usually includes plenty of aunts and uncles that are willing baby-sitters for young pups. In all, I can think of no animal that deserves less to be shot and more to be preserved.

Another Cascade predator I admire and am still hoping to spot in the wilderness is the cougar. This great cat *(Felis concolor),* also known as the mountain lion, grows as large as eight feet long and lives on the abundant deer population. Its favorite hunting technique is a seemingly lazy but deadly one: the cat crouches on a tree limb, and then drops like a falling shadow on an unsuspecting animal passing below on a game trail. Like the other great predators native to these forests, the cougar has been either shot off or simply pushed aside by man in the name of civilization or industrial development. And in my opinion, the land has been left much the worse.

Another example of man's negative effect on the wilderness appeared beneath the wing of our Cessna as we swept over the heavily eroded summit of Glacier Peak. Below us, in the valley of a creek running eastward from the mountain into Lake Chelan, lay the ghost town of Holden and its old copper mine, abandoned in 1957. Now I saw from the air what I had not fully appreciated a week before, when I had hiked past the mine on the ground—the immense, ugly object lesson that Holden presents. Downstream from a cluster of old mine buildings, a great yellow stain spread out on the valley floor. The stain was made up of mine tailings—rock excavated from the shafts, processed to remove valuable ores, then discarded onto the landscape.

The mine had first been discovered back in 1887, when the Great Northern Railroad explored this valley as a possible route west to tidewater, and a survey engineer named J. H. Holden noticed a large outcropping, stained reddish brown by iron oxide, on the north side of what came to be known as Copper Peak. Forty years of civilized progress later, the Howe Sound Company, whose geologists had rediscovered the ore body, began burrowing zealously and profitably into the mountain for copper, zinc and precious metals. Twenty years after that, during a decline in the price of copper, Howe Sound abandoned the mine, having extracted—among other metals—600,000 ounces of gold. A contractor removed the mining concern's valuable equipment. But a subcontractor went broke trying to dismantle the mill and other buildings, and their hulks remain to this day.

A summer tapestry of blue lupine, white bistort and crimson Indian paintbrush blooms luxuriantly in a meadow at the bottom of a glacial trough in Mount Rainier National Park.

The tailings also remain: 2.6 million cubic yards of finely crushed rock, spread 100 feet deep over 67 acres. What looks from the air like a huge scar on the wilderness is really something worse—a running sore. The tailings contain traces of cyanide, one of the chemicals used in precipitating ore from rock. Though most of the cyanide has leached into the ground, the Bureau of Mines has had little success in efforts to grow grass here, even with copious applications of ground-sweetening lime and fertilizer. Other residue from the mine causes further problems to the few people in the area, where a Lutheran Church camp has taken over some of the mine buildings. When the wind blows, the village and the valley below are enveloped in clouds of fine, golden-yellow iron-oxide dust. The wound inflicted by the Holden mine is taking a long time to heal, as do all wounds to wild places, whether they are from miners poisoning the earth or hunters killing off its creatures.

In the last decade or so, there have been several countermeasures to ensure that disasters such as Holden—or any other kind of encroachment on the wilderness—do not happen again. Despite bitter opposition from timber operators and other land developers, the federal government has set aside 2,568 square miles of the North Cascades as primitive land that cannot be further violated. The 725-square-mile Glacier Peak Wilderness was established in 1960, the 1,053-square-mile North Cascades National Park in 1968, and the rolling 790-square-mile Pasayten Wilderness, east of the park, was also established in 1968. More parks and wilderness areas are in varying stages of proposal and debate.

Turning our Cessna to the west, Stewart and I flew past the jagged Picket Range. At other times I had been at the foot of these granite peaks on the ground, and they had seemed infinitely high and unscalably steep. From the air they still looked as sharp as shark's teeth as they thrust up through a pool of low clouds. But they now appeared fairly small compared to other, higher mountaintops nearby. Rough-cut Mount Shuksan passed below us and then, at 11,000 feet, we soared around and across Mount Baker.

When we skimmed by, the summit of Baker was almost close enough for me to drag a hand in the snow and to whiff the gases wisping out of yellowed fumaroles—steaming-hot wells—that dot the crater. As I looked down, a day from long ago flashed before my mind: I had been skiing somewhere down there on Mount Baker, in cloudy weather. Quite suddenly, the clouds had lifted to reveal Mount Shuksan and the Picket peaks. Their grandeur distracted me, and I took a long tumble in

Balancing on tiny hooves, a baby mountain goat in its first summer looks for browse among bare boulders above the forest line. In this brutal environment, more than a third of all kids may perish in their first year.

the snow. Today they were barely less distracting in their beauty.

As we flew down the western edge of the range, the shadow of Stewart's plane skipped over miles of eroded rubble that has washed toward the sea. In the places where these gravel sediments were not exposed to our view, they lay masked by the green growths of forests and fields. Glacier Peak, austere and remote in the late-afternoon sun, came and went on our left; then we were over the vast flat delta of the Skagit River. Out there my father and I used to hunt ducks in the rainy dawns' early light, and in the cut-over foothills to the east, we used to take turns doing what we called riding shotgun: one of us would sit back on the tonneau of a touring car while the other drove, trying to scare up and shoot ruffed grouse.

The Cessna now passed over more moraine lakes hanging on the bottom ends of mountain valleys. We wheeled once more around the stubby monument of Mount Si, made a low pass over 300-foot-high Snoqualmie Falls, and then we came in for a landing back at Bellevue.

Summer was now ended. But the following week I decided there was time for one more weekend in the Cascades. Accordingly, Mary and I shouldered our backpacks and headed for a favorite retreat of ours, not far from the summit of Rainy Pass. An hour of up-and-down walking along a muddy path through groves of hemlocks and firs, all sagging and dripping from an afternoon rain, took us to our goal, Lake Ann.

At the near end of the lake, small alders and vine maples grew on fairly flat land at the water's edge. On the other three sides, talus slopes rose abruptly from the shore to the bases of cliffs that formed a high, horseshoe-shaped wall around the lake. Snow covered most of the rockpiles and, at the far end of the lake, two snowmelt waterfalls, still bright at twilight, plunged down from a mountain.

We decided to spend the night by the shore. Mary gathered some firewood, then silently gestured toward a snowbank a few hundred yards away. Two marmots, big as beavers, were playing tag there, whistling and chasing each other across the snow, hiding and reappearing in the rocks, ignoring us completely.

After dinner we spread our sleeping bags near our fire, and as it died down, we went to sleep with the sound of the waterfalls coming across the lake in a steady *sshhh*. A silent, intermittent drizzle fell during the night but it did not bother us; we were dry and snug under the same tarpaulin that had served so well in the storm at Hart Lake.

By morning the waterfalls were mere trickles; it would take hours of sunshine to melt enough snow on the heights above to activate them

again. As we packed to leave, we looked skyward and saw the perfect arch of a rainbow in front of the mountain—and then we also saw a speck of white against a tiny green patch of alpine meadow. Through the binoculars we could see that it was a mountain goat, an adult billy with short black horns and a long, clean coat. He was feeding alone up there in tender grass just a step away from a precipice. He held still for a few moments and then bounded out of sight.

Smaller than a deer, the mountain goat, like so many other wilderness beasts, is remarkably well adapted to its lofty environment. Its soft, flowing white wool is perfect camouflage against the almost year-round snow; and the wool also serves as insulation against the high-mountain cold. The goat's hooves have soft pads that help it climb and hang onto sharp rock ledges where not even a toehold seems possible.

These wild goats are fairly common in the North Cascades: perhaps 7,000 of them live in the high country of Washington state alone. They are shy, but not too hard to find, only hard to see from far away. Some of their favorite haunts are among the lower cliffs of Mount Si, where they bound from one narrow shelf to the next with a magnificent sense of grace and balance.

That afternoon, while we were walking back down the trail, I knew the time had come when I had to leave the Cascades. I felt a sharp longing; all my senses were telling me to stay, that I belonged in this part of the world. The thought of departure was such a wrench that I felt a bodily ache. My efforts to recapture and enlarge the personal meaning of these mountains had not been in any way fruitless; but they had not left me entirely satisfied either. For every black cave I had descended there were dozens more, perhaps even more exciting, left undiscovered and uncrawled. For every peak I had stood upon there were so many, many still to be climbed. For every alpine lake and mountain stream whose waters I had waded or sipped, there were scores of others, unseen and unsavored. And for every cedar tree I had brushed past, every cocky bird I had looked in the eye, there were millions left untouched and unmet—until God knew when. I had to leave, and it saddened me.

This summer in the Cascades, after so many years spent too far away, had taught me something about myself. I like to think of myself as young for my age, and full of curiosity and resiliency; if that is true, it is not only thanks to the happenstance of ancestors and genes. It comes, I think, from growing up at the edge of the wilderness, free to explore, to fill the eyes with the everlasting grandeur of the mountains and to fill the lungs with clean, forest-scented air. And also free to be challenged, to test the leg muscles and the nerve on long hikes to places like Eagle Falls and on longer, higher trips up into the everlasting snows. I was fortunate in my youth and am fortunate now to have the desire and the ability to spend so much time in the Cascades. That desire has become as strong as anything I have ever felt. It pulls me back toward those mountains as insistently as Shangri-la ever tugged at another prisoner of place who came to regret his escape.

Some day, defying the notion that you can't go home again, I shall simply go along with this magnetic force of yearning, even if I have to walk the 3,000 miles home. There would be time, that way, to decide which part of home to head for. Hyas Lake, perhaps, hanging still and blue as a painting below Cathedral Rock. Or some remaining piece of virgin forest, miles into the woods and protected from any logger's chain saw; quiet enough to echo the squawks of woodpeckers, or perhaps even the drip of raindrops.

Or I might head for the rim of Crater Lake, if I were to arrive at a time when I could sense—as John Wesley Hillman did a century ago —that I was the only person looking down into the depths of that great, round blue eye of water. I did look down into Crater Lake on a recent winter day from an airliner at 17,000 feet, and saw it all white-walled with snow and colored the palest innocent blue. The desire to be down there or just *anywhere* back in the Cascades was instantly overwhelming. And I am going to succumb. One day, not long from now, I know I will be back. And whether I walk or ride or fly, I am indeed going to use the whole trip of thousands of miles to decide which part of the Cascades to revisit first. The journey will be a long one, and the choice hard. But what a delightful way to go back home.

Secrets of a Snowbound Fortress

PHOTOGRAPHS BY HARALD SUND

Formidable enough in summer, the Cascades in winter become almost impenetrable—a grim fortress of ice-bound mountain walls and snow-clogged forests. Trails vanish under annual snowfalls of up to 500 inches, and passes are shut by drifts. Winds howl through the valleys and around the peaks, swirling the snow into jutting cornices and plastering it up against tree trunks. Landmarks disappear. Within minutes, a sudden blizzard or a whiteout from fog and wind-blown snow crystals can completely obliterate a sunny day, cutting visibility to a few feet.

Yet to those who breach these obstacles, the Cascades present some of their finest facets—as shown in this portfolio by photographer Harald Sund, who explored the snowbound North Cascades afoot and by light plane over the course of a winter. No aviator by temperament, Sund remembers vividly his airborne approach to the Picket Range: "It was some of the roughest terrain I have ever seen—wave after wave of peaks. The pilot went straight for the peaks and veered off only three hundred yards away. I had to watch the scenery go by through the camera and I started shooting out of fear, just to occupy my mind."

Much happier on the ground and firmly footed on snowshoes, Sund walked alone for miles through the mountains, sometimes camping out for three days at a stretch. In his wanderings he came upon such quiet fascinations as the lacework tracks of a weasel, and basketball-sized sunballs *(page 166)*—chunks of sun-warmed snow that had broken off from a cornice and ballooned as they rolled downhill. He caught fleeting moments of drama, as when the sun broke through the lowering overcast to spotlight a hillside covered with firs and hemlocks *(right)*. And early one evening, Sund earned a special dividend.

He had been shooting since dawn, in an alpine bowl beneath Nooksack Ridge. As the sun set behind him, he aimed his camera toward the spot where he knew the moon must rise, and waited in a cold silence broken only by the crunch of snow underfoot. In a sky bright with alpenglow, the moon gave no forewarning of its rise; it just appeared, and in a moment seemed to dominate the sky. Entranced, Sund kept shooting the play of moonlight on the ridge until long past midnight, when the moon, commencing to set, began drifting down across the western sky.

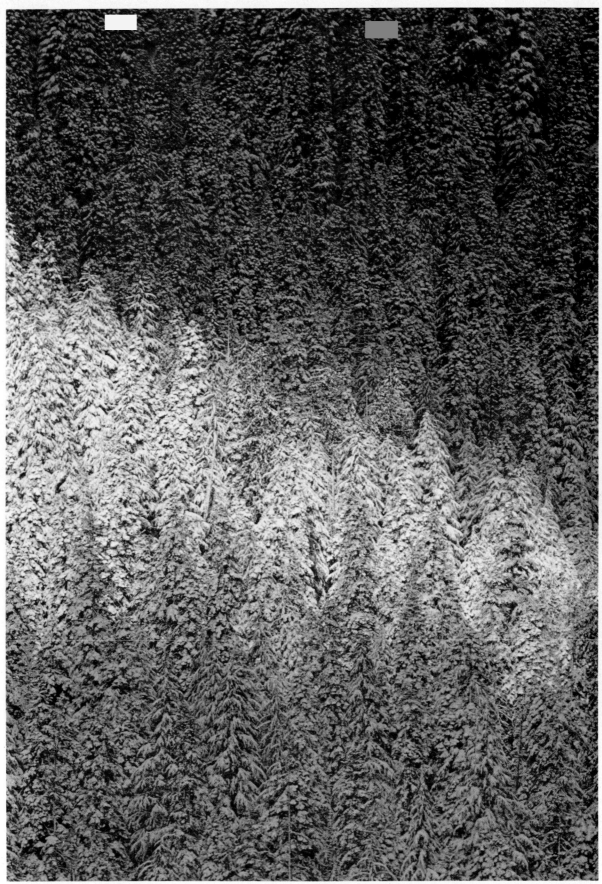

A FLASH OF SUN ON A HILLSIDE NORTH OF SNOQUALMIE PASS

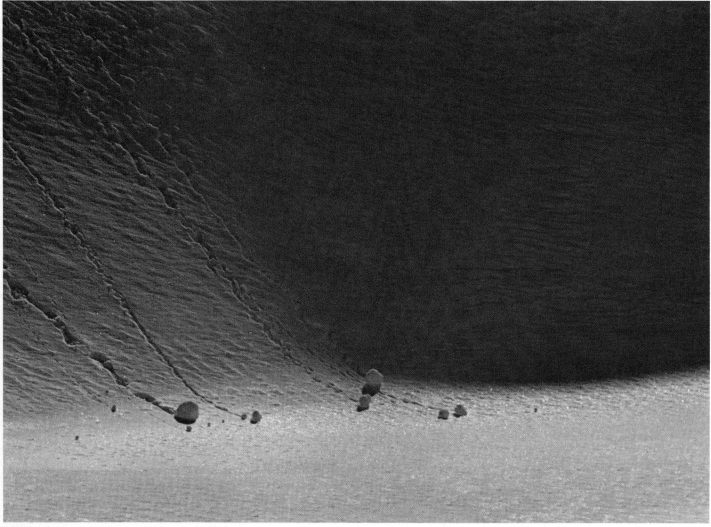

SUNBALLS IN THE FOOTHILLS OF MOUNT BAKER

MOONRISE OVER NOOKSACK RIDGE

AN ALDER THICKET ETCHED AGAINST THE SNOW

CLOUDS GRAZING A RIDGE AT CASCADE PASS

FOG-SHROUDED FIRS ON MOUNT RAINIER

A STAND OF VIRGIN FIR, HEAVY WITH SNOW

SHADED RAVINES BELOW MOUNT BAKER

A RAGGED, FURROWED SUMMIT IN THE PICKET RANGE

HEMLOCKS PLASTERED WITH WIND-BLOWN SNOW

WEASEL TRACKS BELOW THE CROWN OF TABLE MOUNTAIN

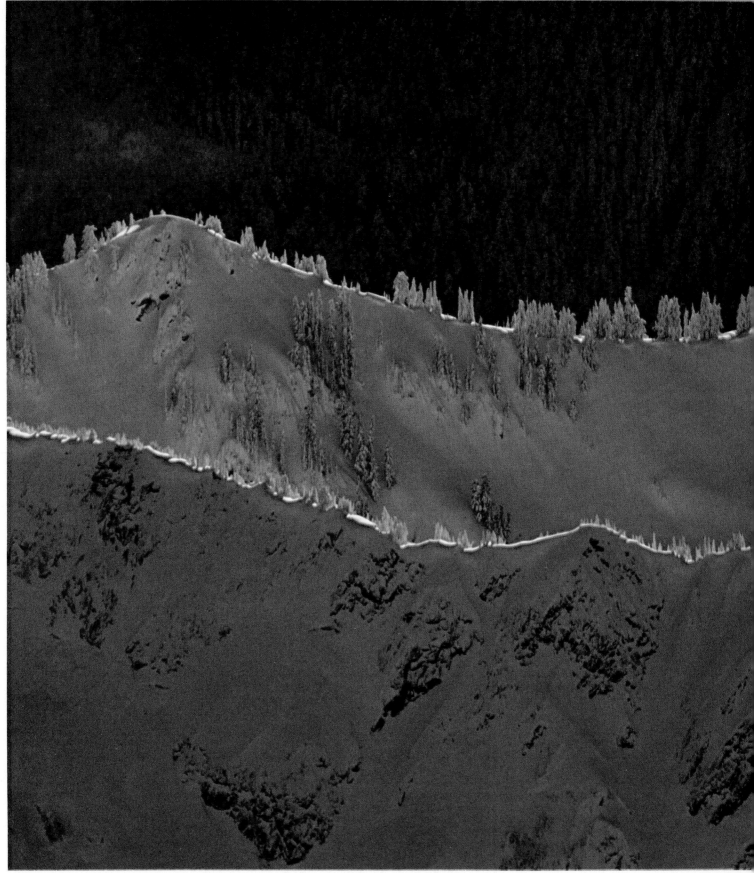

SUN GLOWING ON RIDGES NEAR GLACIER PEAK

Bibliography

*Also available in paperback.
†Available only in paperback.

Atkeson, Ray, *Northwest Heritage, the Cascade Range.* Charles H. Belding, 1969.

†Berry, James Berthold, *Western Forest Trees.* Dover Publications, Inc., 1966.

†Brogan, Phil F., *Visitor Information Service Book for the Deschutes National Forest.* U.S. Department of Agriculture, 1969.

Case, Robert Ormond and Victoria, *Last Mountains: The Story of the Cascades.* Binfords & Mort, 1945.

Douglas, William O., *My Wilderness: The Pacific West.* Doubleday & Company, Inc., 1960.

Eichorn, A. F., *The Mt. Shasta Story.* Privately printed, 1957.

Evans, Brock, *The Alpine Lakes.* The Mountaineers, Seattle, Washington, 1971.

Farner, Donald S., *The Birds of Crater Lake National Park.* University of Kansas Press, 1952.

Federal Writers' Project, *Mount Hood.* Duell, Sloan and Pearce, 1940.

Federal Writers' Project, *Oregon, End of the Trail.* Binfords & Mort, 1951.

Federal Writers' Project, *Washington: A Guide to the Evergreen State.* Binfords & Mort, 1941.

†Franklin, Jerry F., and Norman A. Bishop, *Notes on the Natural History of Mount Rainier National Park.* The Mt. Rainier Natural History Association, no date.

*Franzwa, Gregory M., *The Oregon Trail Revisited.* Patrice Press, Inc., 1972.

*Fries, Mary A., *Wildflowers of Mount Rainier and the Cascades,* The Mt. Rainier Natural History Association, 1970.

*Haines, Aubrey L., *Mountain Fever: Historic Conquests of Rainier.* Oregon Historical Society, 1962.

Haskin, Leslie L., *Wild Flowers of the Pacific Coast.* Binfords & Mort, 1967.

Hosmer, James K., *History of the Expedition of Lewis and Clark.* 2 vols. A. C. McClurg & Company, 1902.

Ingles, Lloyd G., *Mammals of the Pacific States.* Stanford University Press, 1965.

Jackman, E. R., and R. A. Long, *The Oregon Desert.* The Caxton Printers, Ltd., 1971.

†Larrison, Earl J., *Washington Mammals: Their Habits and Distribution.* The Seattle Audubon Society, 1970.

Lavender, David, *Land of Giants.* Doubleday & Company, Inc., 1958.

*Lavender, David, *Westward Vision: The Story of the Oregon Trail.* McGraw-Hill Book Company, 1963.

*McKee, Bates, *Cascadia: The Geologic Evolution of the Pacific Northwest.* McGraw-Hill Book Company, 1972.

Manning, Harvey, *The North Cascades.* The Mountaineers, Seattle, Washington, 1964.

*Manning, Harvey, *The Wild Cascades: Forgotten Parkland.* Sierra Club, 1969.

†May, Allan, *Up and Down the North Cascades National Park.* The Mt. Rainier Natural History Association, 1973.

Meany, Edmond S., *Mt. Rainier, a Record of Exploration.* Binfords & Mort, 1916.

Muir, John, *Steep Trails.* Houghton Mifflin Company, 1918.

Murray, Keith A., *The Modocs and Their War.* University of Oklahoma Press, 1959.

†Osborne, Kelsie Ramsey, *Peaceful Conquest: Story of the Lewis and Clark Expedition.* Beattie & Company, 1955.

Peattie, Donald Culross, *A Natural History of Western Trees.* Houghton Mifflin Company, 1953.

Peattie, Roderick, ed., *The Cascades.* Vanguard Press, 1949.

Peck, Morton Eaton, *A Manual of the Higher Plants of Oregon.* Binfords & Mort, 1961.

†Sharpe, Grant and Wenonah, *101 Wildflowers of Crater Lake National Park.* University of Washington Press, 1959.

Spring, Bob and Ira, and Harvey Manning, *The Key to Our Environment . . . Cool, Clear Water.* Superior Publishing Company, 1970.

†Sudworth, George B., *Forest Trees of the Pacific Slope.* Dover Publications, Inc., 1967.

Thornbury, William D., *Regional Geomorphology of the United States.* John Wiley and Sons, Inc., 1965.

†Whitwar, Donald H., *Visitor Information Service Reference Book of the Mt. Hood Area.* 2 vols. U.S. Department of Agriculture, 1965.

†Williams, Howel, *The Geology of Crater Lake National Park, Oregon.* Carnegie Institution of Washington, Publication 540, 1942.

Winther, Oscar Osburn, *The Old Oregon Country,* Stanford University Press, 1950.

*Yocom, Charles, and Vinson Brown, *Wildlife and Plants of the Cascades.* Naturegraph Publishers, 1971.

Bulletins and Professional Papers

Coombs, Howard A., *Mt. Baker, a Cascade Volcano.* Geological Society of America, 1939.

Coombs, Howard A., and Arthur D. Howard, *Catalogue of the Active Volcanoes of the World, Part IX, United States of America.* International Volcanological Association, 1960.

Crandell, Dwight R., *The Geologic Story of Mount Rainier.* U.S. Government Printing Office, 1969.

Crandell, Dwight R., *Postglacial Lahars from Mount Rainier Volcano, Washington.* U.S. Government Printing Office, 1971.

Crandell, Dwight R., *Surficial Geology of Mount Rainier National Park, Washington.* U.S. Government Printing Office, 1969.

Crandell, Dwight R., and Donal R. Mullineaux, *Recent Lahars from Mount St. Helens, Washington.* U.S. Government Printing Office, 1962.

Acknowledgments

The author and editors of this book are particularly indebted to James Anderson, Bend, Oregon. They also wish to thank the following. In Oregon: Edwin B. Abbott, Rogue River National Forest, Medford; Philip Brogan, Bend; Luther S. Cressman, Professor Emeritus of Anthropology, University of Oregon, Eugene; Samuel T. Frear, Willamette National Forest; Carl Gohs, Portland; Milton J. Griffith, Deschutes National Forest, Bend; James Holcomb, Crater Lake National Park, Crater Lake; James Hughes, U.S. Forest Service, Portland; Mr. and Mrs. Richard B. Kreuzer, Sunriver; Frank A. Lang, Associate Professor of Biology, Southern Oregon College, Ashland; James Morries, Columbia Gorge Ranger Station, Troutdale; Warren Olney, U.S. Forest Service, Zigzag; The Oregon Historical Society, Portland; Merle F. Pugh, U.S. Forest Service, Portland; Ray Schaaf, Rogue River National Forest, Medford; Terry Virgin, Deschutes National Forest, Bend; Richard Woodrow, Mount Hood National Forest, Portland; Lester Yates, Deschutes National Forest, Bend. In Washington: Charles F. Banko, Leavenworth Ranger Station, Leavenworth; J. Christopher Comstock, Wenatchee National Forest, Chelan; Howard A. Coombs, Professor of Geology, University of Washington, Seattle; Robert C. Cunningham, North Cascades National Park, Sedro Woolley; Alan Eliason, North Cascades National Park, Sedro Woolley; Jack H. Hyde, Instructor in Geology, Tacoma Community College, Tacoma; Arthur Kruckeberg, Chairman and Professor of the Department of Botany, University of Washington, Seattle; Stewart Lowther, Professor of Geology, University of Puget Sound, Tacoma; Bates McKee, Affiliate Professor of Geology, University of Washington, Seattle; Peter Misch, Professor of Geology, University of Washington, Seattle; Austin Post, U.S. Geological Survey, Tacoma; William and Margaret Stark, Leavenworth; Bob Stevens, Mount Baker National Forest, Bellingham; James Tobin, Superintendent, Mount Rainier National Park, Longmire; Harry Wills, Mount Rainier National Park, Longmire. And also Don Despaine, Yellowstone National Park, Wyoming; James Doherty, New York Zoological Park, New York City; Sidney S. Horenstein, Department of Invertebrate Paleontology, The American Museum of Natural History, New York City; John Krambrink, Lava Beds National Monument, Tule Lake, California; Larry G. Pardue, New York Botanical Garden, New York City; Clark T. Rogerson, Senior Curator, Cryptogamic Botany, New York Botanical Garden, New York City; Robert Tribble, Shasta-Trinity National Forest, California.

Picture Credits

The sources for the pictures in this book are shown below. Credits for the pictures from left to right are separated by semicolons.

Cover—David Cavagnaro. Front end papers 2, 3—Gary Braasch. Front end paper 4, page 1—Barry Lopez. 2 through 5—Harald Sund. 6, 7—William Garnett. 8, 9—Jerry Y. Takigawa. 10 through 13—Harald Sund. 18, 19—Maps by Hunting Surveys Limited. 23—Ed Cooper. 26—Bob Gunning. 29—Bob Gunning. 33 through 43—William Garnett. 48—Ed Cooper. 50, 51—David Cavagnaro. 54, 55, 56—Ed Cooper. 58—The New-York Historical Society. 62 through 75—David Cavagnaro. 80, 81—Harald Sund. 84—Harald Sund. 87—California Historical Society, San Francisco. 91—U.S. Geological Survey. 92, 93—Far West Aerial Scenes, Tacoma, Washington; Russ Lamb. 94, 95—Russ Lamb; Far West Aerial Scenes, Tacoma, Washington. 96, 97—Ed Cooper. 98 through 101—Harald Sund. 104, 105—Gary Braasch. 108—Ed Cooper. 110—Warren Garst from Tom Stack & Associates. 112, 113—Bob Gunning. 117—Milt Griffith. 121 through 131—Harald Sund. 136 through 147—Harald Sund. 153—Gary Braasch except top left and bottom right Donald Carlson. 154—W. T. Hall from Bruce Coleman, Inc. 158, 159—Bob Gunning. 160—Alan G. Nelson. 165 through 179—Harald Sund.

Index